TURNING FEAR TO HOPE

Women Who Have Been Hurt for Love

TURNING FEAR TO HOPE

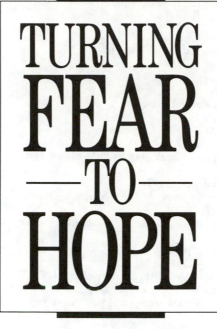

Holly Wagner Green

PYRANEE BOOKS

Zondervan Publishing House
Grand Rapids, Michigan

Turning Fear to Hope
Copyright © 1989 by Holly Green

Pyranee Books
are published by
Zondervan Publishing House
1415 Lake Dr., S.E.
Grand Rapids, MI 49506

Library of Congress Cataloging-in-Publication Data

Green, Holly Wagner, 1947–
    Turning fear to hope / Holly Wagner Green.
        p. cm.
        Reprint. Originally published: Nashville : T. Nelson Publishers,
c1984.
        Bibliography: p.
        ISBN 0-310-44541-8
        1. Abused wives—Pastoral counseling of. 2. Church work with
abused wives. 3. Wife abuse—United States. 4. Abused wives—
Services for—United States. 5. Abused wives—Psychology. I.
Title.
    [BV4445.5G74 1989]   88–13807
    362.8'3—dc19   CIP

Unless otherwise noted, Scripture quotations are taken from *The
New King James Version,* copyright © 1979, 1980, 1982 by Thomas
Nelson, Inc., Publishers.

Scripture quotations from *The Jerusalem Bible, The New American
Standard Bible,* and *The Holy Bible: New International Version* are
used by permission.

Edited by Nia Jones

Printed in the United States of America

89 90 91 92 93 94 95 / CH / 10 9 8 7 6 5 4 3 2 1

To Howard,
my best friend

Contents

Acknowledgments

I wish to express deep gratitude to those whose efforts contributed to the writing of this book:

To Jean and Beth and the other unnamed battered women who have helped bring to life the issue raised here. Their eagerness to be of help to other battered women is a true testimony of their Christian maturity and love.

To the staff of The Salvation Army Social Service Center (Indianapolis, Indiana), who, because of their genuine concern for battered women, thoughtfully gave their support to the project. This book would not have been possible without their cooperation.

To the women in my Bible study group at Walnut Grove Chapel in Indianapolis, to whom I first confessed my desire to write such a book, who offered their encouragement, their prayers, and their interest in the project.

To my husband, Howard, who supported me through it all. He produced a steady stream of background and resource material for me to study, graciously accepted my emotional highs and lows during the writing, and consistently encouraged me. He also edited, proofread, sometimes typed, and gave invaluable advice and constructive criticism.

To my sons David and Daniel, who for the past year have put up with my absentminded, half-hearted housekeeping and cooking. They never complained at being dragged along to the library several times a week and respectfully tiptoed around the typewriter to avoid disturbing me.

Thank you all very much.

Prologue

Two years ago I presented a marriage communication workshop at a women's retreat in the Midwest. The women who participated in the workshop represented various denominations but were for the most part evangelicals.

Midway through the session, a petite blonde hesitantly stood up. "My name is Jean," she said. "I'm leaving my husband to go and live with my mother. For the four years we have been married, my husband has beaten me whenever he has been upset about anything—his work, the car, what we were having for dinner. And I've always taken it. I felt I should put up with it because of my Christian commitment. But the last time he started punching and kicking me, I was holding our baby daughter. He could have killed her." Her shaky voice rose. "Beating up me was one thing. But he was going to hurt my baby."

After a brief, shocked silence had given us all a chance to absorb her words, two other women in the circle spoke up.

"You shouldn't leave your husband," said one. "No matter what he does to you, God put him in charge of you. He's God's responsibility. If something he does to you displeases God, then it's up to God to stop him, not you."

"That's right," the other woman added. "God made him your lord and master. Even if he tells you to jump out the window, you should do it. If God wants you and your baby to live, don't worry. He'll protect you somehow."

Jean turned to me, her face reflecting remembered agonies.

"Did I do wrong?" she asked.

I found myself utterly at a loss. I based my own life on the authority of Scripture and could not deny that the Bible advocates commitment of mate to mate, permanence of the marriage relationship, husbandly headship, and wifely submission. Yet I knew those two women were wrong.

After the retreat I discussed Jean with my husband, Howard. As a marriage and family counselor and the administrator of an evangelical social service agency, he grapples with these same issues.

Does a husband's headship confer on him the authority to hurt, even kill, his wife? Must she submit to this mistreatment? Does the teaching of Scripture force the counselor to tell a battered woman she must stay in the relationship, suffering "for righteousness' sake"? Does the permanence of the marriage bond preclude any separation?

Jean's story prompted me to study the secular literature on domestic violence. I spoke at length with members of my husband's staff, talked to battered women, and listened to taped interviews with their husbands. Howard and I delved into Scripture looking for answers. The result is this book.

I wrote it for Jean because she needed someone to understand and comfort her, someone to help her clarify her thinking. She needed a fellow Christian to search with her through the Word and stand by her during the decision making, during the awful months of vacillating between love and hate, rage and fear, resignation and indignation.

I wrote it for the women who gave Jean misguided advice. Their comments made me aware that there are people who have all the "answers" and no empathy.

I wrote it for Jean's family and friends who wanted to help her and for me and people like me who are sometimes in the position of being asked, "What should I do? What does the Bible say about it?" I wrote it for those who may be the battered woman's last hope before abandoning herself to despair.

Holly Wagner Green

1

Wife Abuse—A True Story

FROM BETH

Funny, the thing I remember most is the summer sun burning my cheek, making the marks left by George's hand feel redder than ever. As I stumbled from one street to the next, I fingered my aching jaw and tried to make sense of the incident. I'd been Mrs. George Lansing for less than a week and already I was feeling hurt, uncertain, and afraid.

A lot about those early years I can't remember at all, but that scene, twenty-five-years-old now, is etched in my mind with the clarity of a photograph.

My dear father had died two months before. If he had lived, I might still have married George eventually, but certainly not when I did—at eighteen. I had loved Dad so much I could hardly face the fact that he was gone. He had been the head of our home in the very best sense, always calm, always ready with the logical solution to any problem, always loving toward us. He never raised his voice that I can remember. He didn't have to. Out of sheer devotion to him, we were eager to do whatever he asked.

After he died, while I was still feeling the loss very deeply, George called me from New Jersey, where he was stationed in the service, and told me to come for a visit. "Maybe, if you're good, we'll get married while you're here," he said. We'd been going together off and on for the past three years, and his unexpected phone call seemed like a miracle. I thought George would comfort me and make me forget how I missed Dad.

On the morning of that first awful incident, he had announced that he was going to the base to play softball with his friends.

"But we're on our honeymoon," I called after him as he went out the door. "Can't I at least come along?"

"Just stay put." He offered no other explanation.

I didn't think this was how it was supposed to be. Newlyweds spent all their time together—happy, completely and wonderfully happy. What had I done to displease him? Why didn't he want me with him? Fear and doubt prickled at the back of my neck. I tried to occupy myself cleaning and scrubbing, and I concentrated hard to keep out the hurt and the loneliness until a neighbor at the trailer court called and invited me shopping. We ended up at a snack bar where I spent fifty cents on a Coke and a sandwich.

George was home by late afternoon, looking gritty and tired from his game. He flopped onto the sofa, one leg over the arm, his head thrown back. I told him that Mary and I had been out for lunch. In the blink of an eye he was on his feet. He screamed at me for spending his hard-earned money. He said I had no business going off like that by myself and how dare I think I could.

I was so shocked I could not really take it in. What in the world was all the fuss about? My stomach knotted as I looked up into his angry face. I must not have apologized quickly enough because he grabbed me by the throat and shoved me up against the kitchen wall, banging my head against it with such force that I saw stars. The attack was so sudden I didn't have time to cry out.

"You'd better shape up, little girl," he growled at me. "You'd better mend your ways or there is going to be fur flying around here." With a stinging slap across the face to teach me my lesson, he stormed out, slamming the door behind him.

My head roaring, my cheek blotched red, I ran out, too. For the rest of the afternoon I wandered about in the stifling heat, humiliated, ashamed, and afraid. What should I do? Where could I go? Small groups of strangers jostled past me as I stood on the sidewalk, their carefree laughter coming to me from a great distance. Everyone looked blurry through my tear-swollen eyes.

There was no place for me to go in that strange city, so eventually I went back to the trailer.

When I pushed open the door, he was there, concerned and apologetic. Where had I been? Was I all right? He was so sorry. He would never behave like that again. Could I ever forgive him?

What a question! Of course I could. I loved him, didn't I? Everything was going to be all right, because we were both nice, respectable people. George and I were both Christians, too. Although his family did not share his faith as mine did, he was definitely a believer. What was there to fear? This incident must have been a fluke, the result of some outside pressure I knew nothing about. Surely it would never happen again.

How wrong I was.

I had always been flattered by George's proprietary ways. He was a tall, handsome young man, his hair thick and curly, his eyes sparkling with laughter. He often walked down the street with his arm around me "to protect you from all those other guys," he'd say. "No one else is going to get my girl." His attentions made me feel like Cinderella until the next of his violent episodes.

It came the week before Christmas. We didn't have much money to spend, but we had fun window shopping and enjoying the storefront decorations. The light posts had big red bows, and silver bells were suspended across the streets. The whole world seemed merry. Even strangers smiled at each other on the sidewalks.

We took scalloped potatoes to a potluck church supper, and I basked in the glow of feeling that I belonged somewhere at last. George bustled from table to table, chatting with friends and greeting newcomers. I watched him, shy myself and proud of the way he was at ease with everybody. I could pick out several families whose names I knew. When they looked over, I waved at them and smiled. A neighbor of ours came over and sat down beside me. At first I didn't know what to say, but he was kind and relaxed. Before I knew it, I was chatting just like everybody else. We laughed and talked for several minutes before I saw George stalking back to the table.

"We're leaving," he said through clenched teeth. With a firm hand on my elbow he marched me out the door. Somehow I knew right away that something serious was about to happen. In a flash, without a word, he grabbed me by the front of my coat, picked me up, and hurled me down into the dirty slush and snow of the parking lot. I scrambled to my feet, embarrassed and sore, but he was not yet finished. He shoved me into the car with all his strength and then punched my side.

"You shouldn't be talking with other men when I'm not around."

"George," I gasped in pain, "why are you doing this? Joe is our friend. What's the matter with you?"

I pleaded and argued all the way home. I knew there were times when I did dumb things, but this wasn't one of them. Righteous indignation momentarily overcame fear. Once my courage was up, it was hard for me to stop. I was not going to let him get away with believing there was anything going on between Joe and me.

"Come on now, George, stop it. Please, stop it."

Tears that I tried to blink back would not be contained. They spilled down my face. "I didn't do anything wrong."

As we walked through the front door of our trailer, out of sight of possible prying eyes, he backhanded me across the face with all his might and then slapped me again.

"Don't cry. Do you hear me? Stop this minute, or I'll really give you something to cry about." His arm swung back and forth, landing first on one side of my face, then on the other. My nose began to bleed, and my eye swelled shut.

As suddenly as he had lashed out, he seemed to realize what he had done. He ran to the kitchen and brought me ice for my eye and a cloth for my bleeding nose, saying, "Oh, no, what have I done? Can you ever forgive me? Oh, my poor baby."

A heavy, dead calm came over me like a blanket. I felt like a rock. I stood still, not crying anymore, not shaking, just staring across the room at the empty wall over the stereo. *We should hang a picture there*, I thought.

Without another word I went to bed. He fussed around me, worrying over my appearance, imploring my forgiveness, searching my face in an attempt to determine what I was thinking, how I was taking this.

I remember thinking, *This will all work out. My face is aching, but I'm actually relieved this happened. Because now he'll stop. Things will be different. I can see the alarm in his face. He's horrified at what he did. This will all work out.*

He woke me at five the next morning, "Beth, you look terrible. What are we going to say?" He was right. My blackened, swollen face was a dreadful sight. His sorrowful eyes melted my heart. I reassured him that I would cover for him.

"Listen, George," I said. "You don't have to worry about that. If I see any of our friends, I'll tell them that when we were driving home last night I had my hands in my pockets, and when you turned the corner I lost my balance and hit my head against the dashboard of the car."

He looked so relieved that I felt very good about protecting him. I didn't want to hurt him or get him into trouble. One look at his anxious expression and my fear subsided. It felt good to be planning something together, to be co-conspirators at covering this up. Bed felt especially cozy as I snuggled into the crook of his arm.

This is nice, I thought. *This is "married." Let it always be like this, Lord.*

It didn't last. As soon as the black around my eye faded to purple and then to yellow, his solicitousness faded, too. Before long we had established a routine. I'd say something or do something, and he'd get mad, scream and yell at me, and then storm out. I was under the strictest control. I could not go out without him. I could not make any decision or spend any money. He chose my clothes. He told me what to do and when to do it. He even did the shopping for me and often told me what to cook and how to fix it. I deeply resented the implication that I didn't know enough to prepare decent meals for him, but when I brought up the issue he would not discuss it.

"I can do this for you myself," I wanted to shout. "I can be a good wife!" But I never did shout it. George was not the type of man you shouted at. *He* did the shouting.

After we had been married a short time, George left the service, and our life took off on a very rocky course indeed. For a while he went into business with his uncle. When that fell through, he seemed unable to find a new direction in life. He began to hop from job to job, never satisfied with the way he was treated, always finding an excuse to quit. We borrowed heavily from his brother to make ends meet. We were expecting our third child when I began to get frantic for some stability.

"George, this isn't right. You must get yourself together. We are the parents of two, almost three, children. It is just plain wrong to rely so much on your brother. Other people make it on their own and we must, too. We can't go on. . . ."

"So, you don't think I'm doing a good enough job of providing for you, is that it? You wish you'd married one of your other boyfriends because they made it big, and you'd be living the life of Riley now instead of scraping by with me. Well, don't you tell me how to run my life. You mind your own business, and let me work things out. Quit your complaining, and don't you ever think *you* are going to give *me* orders!"

He heaved his glass of iced tea at me, and it shattered onto the floor. "There, do your own work. Clean up that mess and leave me alone!"

He pushed me in the direction of the broom closet, and I slipped and fell in the spilled liquid.

"George, please!" My hands and knees were cut by slivers of glass. There was no pain at first, only the sight of blood dripping down and swirling as it mixed with the tea. I was transfixed watching it. Trickles of red changed shape and spread out around me. It was like the time I fell in the rain running to meet my father at the end of the driveway. Only that time I got carried to the house and petted, and I was allowed to put my feet up on the sofa and have ice cream to make me feel better.

George's kick caught me unawares and brought me back to the present. "Shut up that crying. I told you never to cry," he growled and stomped away.

This time there was no apology outright, but later he did insist on checking my hands for glass fragments before I put on the Band-Aids.

"*I'm* the head of this house, Beth," he reminded me as he bent to examine my lacerations. "Don't forget that. As Christ is the head of the church, so the husband is the head of the wife. I love you, but love requires discipline. You have to learn to leave the decision making to me. Don't tell me what to do."

I watched him patiently bandaging my hands and knees just as my dad had done, the curly hair I loved so much falling over his forehead as he worked. Why couldn't I keep my mouth shut? If I could learn my rightful place, I wouldn't need to fear him. This was all my fault.

Over the next few months I continued to blame myself for George's intense rages. The pattern became predictable: First a mistake by me, then a blowup by George. After each explosion he left the house but phoned me within minutes. "Did Mike call? I'm expecting to hear from him today."

I think these phone conversations were meant to gauge my reaction to what he had done, and to make sure I was still there waiting for his return. Perhaps in the beginning it was his way of trying to make amends and let me know the incident was over.

With my relationship to George so precarious, I turned much of my attention to raising our children. George wanted children badly, and we had five, three girls and two boys, one right after the other. Fatherhood was important to him, but it did not include holding, feeding, diapering, or bathing babies. I hoped he would take more interest in them as they grew older, but he never did. I always attended school functions and Little League games without him.

For their part, the children were encouraged to pretend they did not know what was going on between their dad and me. I had made a vow early on never to speak a word against him to them. And I made sure they did not speak a word against him to me. When he was rough with me, they looked away and quickly left the room with fearful, downcast eyes. It did not occur to me to worry about what their fragile little minds were absorbing. I just wanted them out of the way.

Actually I was more concerned about the neighbors than about the children. We had moved to a small house, one of eight crowded onto a street with space for six. I looked directly into my neighbor's kitchen window from my own. That closeness and the paper-thin walls increased my humiliation and embarrassment during George's rampages. But in all the years we lived there, none of the neighbors mentioned the fighting, and no one ever complained about the noise. I guess they decided it was a private thing between us, and they shouldn't get involved. Gradually we saw less and less of them as our "private" problem became more and more obvious in my black eyes, bruises, and shrieks in the night.

As unbearable as life sometimes seemed, I could think of nothing to do about it. For better or for worse, this was it for me. What God had joined together, man dared not put asunder. Leaving George would be unconscionable, not only because of my faith—although that was a big part of it—but also because of my fear. He had me completely in his control. I lived according to his moods. Scowling? Hide. Glum? Offer sympathy and smile. Even when he was happy, my stomach was tight with the worry that something would go wrong.

Prayer helped me through my days. At first I used prayers mechanically—reciting them over and over as if to ward off evil. *Dear God, protect me. Dear Lord, keep me safe.* But as time went on I grew spiritually, and my prayers came to be personal, real, and sustaining. I got up early to pray while the house was quiet. I prayed that the Lord would help me to be a good wife. I couldn't understand why I was failing so miserably. I prayed that the Lord would help George to relax and come to see how hard I was trying. I prayed, "Please, Lord, make things easier on him." I prayed each day that the children would keep out of his way, that they would do all their fussing while he was out of the house. Most of all, I prayed that the Lord would help me conquer my fear.

I put little notes on the refrigerator:

Casting all your cares upon Him,
for He cares for you.

And:

Be anxious for nothing,
but in everything by prayer and supplication,
with thanksgiving, let your requests
be made known unto God.

I read and reread certain psalms until I knew them from memory and could recite them under my breath as I went about my housework. I never lost faith that the Lord could help George and me.

I had many answers to prayer—many days when the children behaved perfectly, days when there were no insults or shouted threats, days without slaps and kicks. But the most memorable answer was the one that brought George his job—his steady job. I had covenanted with the Lord to thank Him in advance for finding work for George. Each day for a month I prayed, "Thank You, dearest Father, that You are right now preparing the job that You have in mind for George." One month to the day after I began this prayer, George came in beaming at supper time, his eyes full of the old sparkle.

"You're looking at the newest member of the best insurance team in the country," he grinned. I could hardly contain my joy. This was it, the Lord's provision for changing our lives to be the way He wanted them to be, full of love and tenderness. How wonderful He was, how glorious, how faithful!

My elated sense of well-being was short-lived, however. Although George now had a steady job, one he seemed to enjoy, his behavior at home did not improve. Instead it got worse.

Could it be the long hours, the pressure of keeping his output up? Could it be the time he spent away from us on the road? Could it be the new feeling of importance, the free lunches with clients, the expense account? I didn't know, but whatever it was, it further ravaged our relationship. My attempts to personify the loving, submissive wife seemed to stimulate him to treat me worse. His language became incredibly foul. The names he called me, some of them completely unfamiliar, nevertheless made me feel dreadfully humiliated. As insurance work occupied more and more of his life, the part left over for me became increasingly volatile.

He was a different fellow altogether to his friends. Twenty years later, when he had his heart attack and co-workers from the office called to console me, I became aware of a different George.

"George," they told me, "is the greatest guy in the world. Everybody loves him. He's such a happy-go-lucky, carefree character. We can't believe he has had a heart attack. That's just not his style. He's the friendly joker, the life of the party, everybody's pal. He's never in a bad mood, never bothered by anything. How could this happen to him?"

Were they talking about my George? Was this the same man who usually came home bad tempered and spoiling for a fight? Was this the same George who belittled, threatened, and cursed me with such regularity? They didn't know him at all.

Some things in our life together seemed more likely than others to trigger violence, and church attendance was one of them. I developed severely conflicting feelings toward Sunday mornings. On the one hand, I desperately needed the spiritual strengthening available from worship. On the other hand, each service was sure to spark an angry outburst.

George was especially uncomfortable at communion. He took it seriously enough that he could not participate in it because of the sin in his life. Leaving church after communion he was like a pressure cooker on a hot stove, sooner or later bound to explode.

"You little hypocrite! How can you take communion? Do you think you're so perfect?" He would lean across the front seat of the car and thump my head with the heel of his hand, knocking me into the window. "Just don't try to be so high and mighty. You're no better than anyone else."

He would drive home too fast, drop the kids and me at the front door, and then head over to his brother's for the afternoon. He simply could not stand the sight of me on Sundays.

Thoroughly intimidated, I tried doubly hard to be the perfect wife. One day he screamed at me that I was a no-good housekeeper, holding up the capless toothpaste tube as Exhibit A. I searched quickly for a way to redeem myself.

"I'm sorry, George, but look! I cleaned up the linen closet today." Of course, I know now that reasoning with him was pointless. In one swipe he knocked the neatly folded stacks of sheets and towels, pillowcases and tablecloths onto the floor in a disheveled heap. Blinking back the tears, I knelt to resort and refold. I have since come to understand that he was not really yelling at me about the housekeeping. He was yelling because it felt good and because I always accepted it.

While on my hands and knees I tried to regain some composure. A memory stirred in a faraway corner of my mind, taking me back to a visit from my mother when I had our first baby. It was the first time she had seen me since my wedding two years before. She must have recognized what was going on even at that early date. Although she never interfered or uttered a word against George, she did say to me casually one day, "You know, Beth, I don't want to butt into your business. But I think that if you stood up to George a bit more he would not run all over you." At the time I did not know what she meant.

And I never got a chance to discuss it with her again. She died quietly in her sleep only a few months later. Now her words returned to me, and I understood. But my fear had grown too strong. I could not follow her suggestion.

"Oh, Mother, Mother, I'm so lonely. I wish I could talk to you now."

Instead, I pursued my course of trying to be everything George wanted. One afternoon I took extra pains getting a special meal ready for him. I shelled fresh peas, scrubbed potatoes and wrapped them in foil for baking, made fancy sauce for the chicken, and even baked a pie. I splurged on a small bouquet of daisies and placed them on the table between two yellow candles.

He arrived home late, his bleak mood evident from the lines on his face. He said nothing about the lovely table and ignored the tantalizing aromas drifting from the stove. I began to feel my usual apprehension as I placed the food in front of him, but still I had hopes of salvaging the occasion.

"What is this?" He speared a baked potato and held it under my nose, his voice deceptively calm and controlled.

"A baked potato," I answered. My eyes were starting to tear, partly from fear and partly from the pain of the scalding foil blistering my nose. I hid my trembling hands in my lap, knowing that shaking and weeping would set him off even more.

"You lazy good-for-nothing!" he shouted. The children, unprepared for the outburst, jumped in their seats, and the littlest ones whimpered.

"Shut up!" The candles and flowers flew off the table as he lashed out at them. In a matter of seconds he had worked himself into a frenzy of anger, calling me such obscene names that I wept at the shame of it. He accused me of being too lazy to mash his potatoes the way he liked them.

He followed me into the kitchen, lunging and jabbing at me with his fists, throwing the flour canister to the floor and then kicking it at me.

"I guess there is nothing I can do about this except to look after my own meals," he shrieked. "I'll eat out." And he was gone.

Late that night, huddled alone and miserable in the bed, I tried to take stock of my life. As much as I wanted to believe that I was getting used to him, that I could handle him on my own and finally win him over, my body had refused to be persuaded, and I was plagued by indigestion, insomnia, palpitations, and shortness of breath. I decided to go for help.

The next morning I slathered makeup over my burned nose and went to our doctor. He prescribed phenobarbital for all my symptoms and told me with a kindly pat on the back that I would be fine. He gave me the tranquilizer without any attempt to find out why I so desperately needed one. I went home with the bottle of artificial calm, determined once more to make everything right for George and me.

The same scenarios repeated themselves through the years. The specifics of many incidents are hazy now, running together in a washed-out blur, but some memories remain crystal clear.

I remember well our friend Frank's fortieth birthday party. We were down in Frank's basement. George and most of the other men were busy playing darts—no women allowed—and we wives were getting bored waiting for them to finish their game.

"Come on over to my house, and I'll show you my craft ideas for vacation Bible school," Sue suggested to a couple of us. It sounded like a good idea. After shouting our good-byes to the men, we all trooped over to Sue's and sat around with coffee for an hour or so talking about children, pets, and vegetable gardens.

Later Sue drove me back to the party, but when we saw George's car was gone she took me home. He was waiting for me. As I climbed the stairs he came charging from the bedroom and stood staring down at me with a terrible, fierce face.

"Who drove you home? Mick? Gary? Who were you with?" he demanded, blocking my way. Before I could answer he jammed his foot into my chest and sent me flying down the full flight of stairs.

Sharon, our daughter, had awakened and come out into the hall to ask me something; she screamed as I fell. She ran down and knelt beside me, alternately sobbing and whimpering. I was numb. Why had he done that? What had I done? Again I felt the desperate need to justify myself, to make him understand that my actions were perfectly innocent. I got up, hushed Sharon and reassured her that I was fine, though I thought I probably had some broken ribs. Starting up the stairs again, I tried to explain. "Listen, George, honey—"

Before I could say more, he had me by the neck and had forced me into the bathroom where I was cornered between the tub and the sink. When I moved toward the door he lunged after me, beating me in the face. I covered my head with my arms as best I could, by this time really frightened he was going to kill me.

"Bitch!" he shrieked. "Slut! Whore!"

Sharon was screaming in the background, but the rest of the children did not appear. Whether they were sleeping so soundly they didn't wake up or whether they were cowering in their beds, I was not to know until later.

His anger spent, George walked away, muttering, "I ought to kill you now and get it over with." I slumped against the tub in a by-now-familiar condition—bruised, sore, aching, and broken in spirit.

I had long since given up making excuses to my friends. Feeling much too low to see anyone anyway, I just hid away. But my best friend stopped by a day or so after that incident and guessed right away what had happened.

"George hit you, didn't he?" she asked matter-of-factly. I didn't lie to her. There was no point in it, and I was too miserable to be concerned about what she might think about me and my marriage.

"I know he treats you like dirt, threatens and belittles you at the drop of a hat. I've heard him call you 'ignorant' and 'stupid' enough times to be sure he must do worse in private," she continued. She didn't offer any advice, and we didn't mention separation or divorce. Marriage was forever—until death. "I pray for you, Beth," she said.

George no longer worried about my reaction to the frequent injuries. He no longer apologized, no longer seemed concerned about what I might say or do. We never discussed what excuse I should give. He knew I was utterly trapped. In fact, the visible aftermath of my beatings awakened in him a new contempt for me.

"Look at you. You're a mess. Why can't you learn? If you hadn't been out when you shouldn't be, none of this would have happened. I still think you were fooling around with someone, and I'd better not find out who it was. You're looking to get yourself killed, girl, and no one in this world can stop me."

I opened my mouth to try once more to exonerate myself but decided it wasn't worth the risk.

This incident depressed and frightened me to such an extent that I made an appointment to see our pastor. I had put it off for years because I had been afraid of damaging George's reputation at church.

Leaning back in his swivel chair, my pastor watched me closely as I related as many details of the relationship as I could remember. His nods of reassurance encouraged me to pour out my hurts and frustrations. When I was finished we sat in silence for a few minutes as he seemed to be marshaling his thoughts.

"Beth, I've seen a number of cases similar to what you are describing here. When I hear this kind of story from a wife who says her husband is abusing her and so on and so on, it usually turns out that it is because she is, you know, provoking him, sticking her chin out. Now while that does not excuse his violence, neither does it excuse her unsubmissive behavior. In most cases, if you start living the way you should—obeying him, being submissive, helping him to feel he's the king of the castle, so to speak—you'll find you get a very different kind of response from him."

My mouth had dropped open a little as his words reached me across the desk. Not a word about George's responsibility in all this. I had expected sympathy, but I seemed to be getting the blame.

"Yes, I know all that." I tried again, "I used to think that I could make things better by doing what you say I should. I really have tried." I told him about the dinner with the baked potato, stressing how hard I had tried to be perfect. "But I've come to believe that no matter what I do he will still hurt me."

"Well, I think we can dismiss that as so much nonsense now, can't we?" he replied, smiling. "We have scriptural assurance that that isn't so." He opened his Bible and read from 1 Peter, " 'Likewise you wives, be submissive to your own husbands, that even if some do not obey the word, they, without a word, may be won by the conduct of their wives, when they observe your chaste conduct. . . . ' You see, Beth, if you behave toward him as you should, he's not going to be able to resist it. A guy just can't take that very long. I guarantee things will change if you adopt this scriptural principle. George will find himself changing whether he wants to or not. 'You're tremendous,' he will say to you some day. 'I don't deserve a wife like you.' "

"I'm not sure how much longer I can go on. It's very scary. He might kill me. Don't you understand how terrified I am?"

He began quoting 1 Peter again. " 'Who is he who will harm you if you become followers of what is good?' and 'But even if you should suffer for righteousness' sake, you are blessed.' You can think of yourself as suffering for your faith. This is what Christ wants you to do. He did it. So can you."

"How am I suffering for my faith?" I asked.

"Beth, you seem pretty upset. I hope you are not trying to get me to tell you it is all right for you to leave George. There is no justification in the Scripture for divorce. Dodge his punches as best you can, but don't ever think I will sanction your separation from George. As you yourself pointed out, George is a believer. You are to stay in your place, trusting your life into the hands of your heavenly Father. All I can suggest to you is that you try harder to be a better wife. It will work. You'll see."

I'd already lived years of trying to be a better wife. George reacted to my behavior by despising me more. His contempt for me grew every day. I could see it in his eyes and in the curl of his mouth when he looked at me. Now, with the church's blessing added to my own acquiescence, the violence intensified. I was convinced that no one could ever make him stop.

My pastor had been my last hope, and after my meeting with him I resigned myself to death at my husband's hands. The doctor increased my phenobarbital prescription and added two other little tablets to my daily intake. My prayers drifted from their early theme of helping George to mere laconic requests that the Lord get me through another day.

Months passed in this manner before a bright stab of pain finally broke through my fog of drugs and despair. Some of the children, as they had gotten older, were also coming under their father's blasts of fury. He had never hit or abused them when they were small, but as they grew up he began to humiliate and torment them—especially Julie, our oldest. The yelling and screaming, the threatening and scolding, penetrated the haze I was in, and I awoke to the seriousness of the situation. His actions toward her stirred me in a way his cruelties to me never had.

She came to me one day, brokenhearted and weeping.

"Mother, how have you been able to stand it? It hurts so much." We sat in silence for a long time before she continued. "You never realized it, but when we were little and Dad would beat you, we hid in the closets, hands over our ears to try to escape the sounds of it. I was terrified for you, and I was scared for me, too—too scared to try to come to your rescue even though I knew I should. It made me feel horrible."

Her stress manifested itself much the same way mine had—physically. She developed an ulcer. I could see the confusion and anxiety on her face and in the stoop of her thin, little shoulders. I had to do something about our life—if not for myself, then for my children.

I wondered for the first time how the other girls had reacted to our strained and precarious lifestyle. What had happened to them deep down inside? Were they growing up to believe all marriages were like mine?

The boys seemed the least affected. Looking back, I see the Lord's hand in it. I would never have thought to encourage them in this direction myself, but what they did, on their own, was to seek out men they admired to be their special friends and role models for adulthood. I suppose they didn't consciously decide to do this, but one turned to the father of a friend and the other to a school guidance counselor. Each went off in his own direction and found the person he needed to be like a father to him. They have turned out to be fine young men, and I give the Lord all the praise for answering my prayers on their behalf.

As the situation with the children was rousing me out of my lethargy, I received another prod from my sister and brother-in-law, who were visiting from Arizona. They were shocked by my emaciated appearance and at George's behavior toward me, which he took no pains to hide.

"We always knew your life with George wasn't easy. But we never knew it was this bad. Why didn't you tell us? Why didn't you come to us? You've been a good wife and a good mother, Beth. You're a wonderful person, and your children are a credit to you. You've kept your strength despite tremendous hardships. Beth, don't you see that all your efforts to please George and adapt to him have failed? That nothing you ever did made any difference? It's no use trying. George needs help you can't give him."

Within days of this discussion George suffered his heart attack. My first thoughts as I looked at him, lying so pale in the hospital bed, were, *Praise the Lord! Surely this will change him. He cannot survive such a terrifying experience without being touched. This is undoubtedly the way the Lord is going to heal our marriage. I won't have to leave him after all.*

As I waited for the miraculous change, I encouraged myself by remembering all the testimonies I had heard and read. Searching for help, answers, and comfort, I had haunted Christian bookstores, devouring accounts of marvelous conversions and restorations, saved marriages, and lives lived happily ever after in Christ. I was primed to expect the supernatural.

There was no miracle for George. He came home from the hospital on a Saturday, and our fragile relationship exploded the very next morning. Things had always been their worst on Sundays, and from the

look on his face as he came to the table for breakfast,
I was sure this Sunday would prove no different.

He surveyed the table with disgust. There was
no currant jelly for his toast. Storming into the pantry
he rifled through the shelves, knocking cereal boxes
and canned goods to the floor. We all sensed his
dangerous mood and held our breaths, afraid to say a
word for fear it would be the wrong one. I kept my
eyes away from him and on the children, watching
them for the least sign that one of them was going to
speak up and make things worse.

"Well, somebody stole my currant jelly," he
bellowed in a moment. "It should be right here and it
isn't. Somebody in this house is a thief. And I can
guess who it is!"

With a roar he swung around and struck me in
the chest with his fist, hurling my chair backward and
flinging me to the floor. I heard and felt my head
crack against the linoleum. The children fled like birds
in all directions. George, momentarily distracted from
his attack, rummaged through the kitchen drawers and
muttered to himself. Dazed and winded, I dragged
myself to the bathroom, the children close behind,
shaken and pale. We huddled there, behind the locked
door, weeping and trying our best to comfort one
another.

George came after us, pounded on the door with
the handle of a large kitchen knife, rattled the knob as
if to tear it off, and even administered a couple of
kicks that cracked the wood.

"Get out of there right now, you bitch. If you
don't, I'll tear you limb from limb. I can kill you and
I will, so help me. If you don't come out, I'll kill the
children, too."

"There, there," I whispered to them. "It's all
right. Everything will be all right." I was trying to
reassure myself as much as them. I remembered my
sister's words, "It's no use trying. George needs help
you can't give."

We stayed in the bathroom for hours, until George gave up his rampage and fell asleep, snoring loudly on the couch. Then we crept out and drove to a motel. The next day I went to a lawyer and through him obtained a restraining order, a legal document prohibiting George from further harassing me and the children.

When George saw it, he was stunned. "What did you do that for? I never hurt you in my life. I'm only trying to make you behave. How could you do this to me?"

Worried for the first time in years, he rushed out and got a lawyer, too, and he took great pains not to bother me or even speak to me. He took a suitcase full of clothes and moved out, demonstrating iron control and the utmost civility. His lawyer had suggested that exemplary behavior would help "his case."

During the days that followed, he frequently drove past our house at night. He also paced up and down the block. Sometimes he was watchful, waiting to catch me with another man—sometimes angry, cursing, threatening, shaking a fist.

Through his lawyer he wrote me nasty letters full of veiled threats. He hinted that if I did not apologize and ask him to come home he would see to it that I lost custody of the children. I endured this for a while and then decided to call his bluff. I'll never know what gave me the courage.

He was out in the yard talking with our two boys one day when I called down to him from an upstairs window.

He looked up, surprised and pleased, assuming, I guess, that I was asking him back.

"You can have custody of the children," I finished.

The change in his expression was instantaneous. His interest in the children had never included taking responsibility for their care, and he certainly didn't want that now.

"Wait, Beth. Let's talk this out," he cajoled as I pulled back from the window. "Beth, don't be hasty. I'm sure we can arrange things to our mutual satisfaction."

No more was said about the children, but he kept up his constant vigil at the house and wore down my nerves with his incessant and obvious presence. Finally, I could bear it no longer. I packed up the children, called my sister, and, as inconspicuously as I could, we left for Phoenix. I stayed there for a year, living with her and her husband and working for the first time in my life. Things were better but not perfect. I worried over the children and felt lonely and unsure. It was not long before George located me. Once he knew where I was, he phoned me at least weekly and even came down to see me.

I know this will sound strange, but it really felt good to see him again, sort of familiar and comfortable. He looked more dear to me than he had in years. We sat down together on the couch. He was quiet, contrite, and tender.

"I'm sorry, Bethie," he said. "I've changed. I can't live without you. I need you and you need me. I want to take care of you and our children. I can't bear to think of you all alone."

For a time there was silence. We sat side by side, each aching with sadness. "We can work this out. It's only a little misunderstanding. You haven't been well. Look how skinny you've gotten. Why don't you concentrate on getting better, maybe put on a little weight, get some rest, then when you feel up to it come on back home to me."

More than anything else in the world I wanted to believe him. I wanted to go back. I wanted to be happily married to him. I wanted my life turned around and straightened out. Because he seemed so sincere and because the children wanted to go home to their friends, too, I relented. George gallantly helped me tie up the loose ends and pack.

Our trip home was interrupted in Missouri when George abruptly announced he was stopping in Kansas City for an insurance conference of some kind. He dropped the five children and me at a small roadside motel out on the highway in the middle of nowhere, then drove into the city to a luxury hotel and partied with his insurance buddies for three days.

"Stay right here and keep out of trouble," he warned me before he left. "I won't be responsible for what happens if you aren't right here waiting when I get back."

Not even home yet and it had begun again! I cried and cried. Things had not changed, and I had placed myself and my children right back into it once more.

My leaving for Phoenix was something George had never expected. He was determined it would never happen again. After he got me back, he warned, "Don't you ever try to escape from me, Beth, because wherever you go, wherever you hide, I'll find you and next time I'll kill you. I swear I will."

There was no doubt in my mind that he meant every word. I realized I was trapped forever.

2

What Is the Problem of Wife Abuse?

Beth's story is by no means unique. Violent relationships are common everywhere in the world, and this country is no exception. Until recently abuse has been a private crime, hidden from public view, its victims shamed or intimidated into silence. When there are witnesses to a husband's assault, they often do nothing to help the victim, feeling that wife beating is a family affair and that they should not become personally involved. It is therefore impossible to collect fully accurate data to demonstrate the actual magnitude of the problem. The truth is, no one knows how many battered women there are. Police reports, court rosters, and social service statistics only reflect the number of cases reported. In fact, law enforcement officials consider abuse to be the single most unreported crime in the United States.

In the 70s, the issue began to emerge from behind closed doors, and since then, increasing numbers of research statistics have accumulated. They confirm that the extent of the problem is staggering.

According to the 1987 American Psychiatric Association figures, nearly four million women are battered in their homes every year, and more than four thousand of them die at the hands of their partners.[1]

The FBI reports that among female murder victims in 1986, thirty percent were slain by husbands or boyfriends.[2]

During 1986, twelve hundred shelters and service programs for victims of abuse across the United States offered sanctuary to 310,000 women and children.[3]

More than a decade ago, a nationwide survey concluded that approximately twenty-eight percent of the couples in this country were involved in abusive relationships. That figure was necessarily low, it was pointed out, as it counted only those willing to come forward.[4] Since then, with the increased publicity surrounding the issue and the increased availability of shelters to house victims, more women are admitting their condition and it has been found that this estimate was indeed conservative. The National Institute of Mental Health now believes that as many as fifty percent of American couples may suffer violence in their marriages.[5]

If you are female, noted domestic violence counselor and researcher Lenore Walker points out, there is one chance in two that you are a battered woman.[6]

It was assumed for years that wife beating occurred only among the poor and disadvantaged. Recent reports, inadequate though they are, help to establish this assumption to be false. For example, in 1974 police in Fairfax County, Virginia, a very wealthy suburb of Washington, D.C., logged 4,073 family disturbance calls. They estimated that thirty assault warrants were requested by wives in the county *each week* of that year.[7]

Interviews with domestic violence counselors confirm that abuse is found in all classes of society. Peihaps the myth that it is confined to the poor arose because police and social service records tend to reflect mostly those cases. Battered middle and upper-class women do not call the police as often or stay in shelters as frequently as their less affluent sisters. They are much more likely to have their own private resources. Furthermore, they may put up with abusive relationships longer. Their lifestyles, their possessions, and their husbands' reputations in the community are at stake if they leave or take legal action against their mates.

Reported or not, abuse transcends all classes and levels of society, all races and ethnic groups, and it affects people of all educational backgrounds. It is a crime that knows no economic or religious boundary. Many evangelicals find it hard to believe that abuse can take place in Christian homes.

"It's a sordid situation, I agree," commented one pastor. "And I don't doubt for a minute that it does exist. But not in my congregation. I would guess that wife abuse is very rare in the evangelical community."

Daniel Keller, an evangelical pastor in Indianapolis, Indiana, has had a different experience. He remarked,

> From talking with my fellow pastors in the area, I would estimate that ten percent of the couples in most evangelical congregations are involved in abusive relationships.
>
> I see a new case of wife battering on the average of once every other month or so within my congregation. These are middle-class church couples—or the extended families of church couples—both generally professing Christians with conservative Christian upbringings.
>
> Every January I preach a short series of sermons on the family, and I make it a point to touch briefly on the topic of wife abuse. I can count on the fact that each year these messages reach several battered women and convince them to come for help.

"How can this be in the Christian family?" asks Wesley Monfalcone, director of chaplaincy services at the University Hospital in Louisville, Kentucky. "Doesn't being a Christian make us different from others who do not experience the grace of God and the fellowship of the church? Yes, it does make a difference. All things are become new in Christ. We are redeemed sinners—but we are sinners yet. Some of the most evil—and foolish—behavior we can observe occurs when religious people believe themselves to be so sanctified that they can do no wrong."[8]

Research data detailing just how many Christian families are involved in abusive relationships are scarce, but it is possible to pull together evidence that the evangelical community is not immune.

The Social Service Center of the Salvation Army in Indianapolis, Indiana, operates a shelter for battered women and a domestic violence counseling program for victims and abusers. The department, staffed entirely by evangelical Christian counselors and social workers, provides service for more than 50 cases of abuse per month (between 300 and 350 new cases each year). Case records for the first six months of 1983 showed that twenty-three percent of the clients seen—nearly one out of every four— were professing Christians affiliated with evangelical churches.

Family Life Today magazine ran several articles on wife abuse in its December 1982 issue and received overwhelming reader response. An editorial note in the April 1983 issue stated, "The relevancy of this topic to our readership was emphasized by the record number of letters sent to us from Christian women who are or have been victims of wife abuse . . . more than we have ever received in response to an article in the magazine."[9]

Religious groups, though not all evangelical, are becoming concerned about this issue and are presenting workshops and training programs to help counselors and pastors prepare to aid victims, abusers, and their children. Recently, the Center for the Prevention of Sexual and Domestic Violence in Seattle began classes specifically for Christian victims of battering, entitled, "Keeping the Faith in the Face of Personal Violence: A Class for Women."[10]

Christian involvement in the prevention and treatment of wife abuse becomes all the more imperative when we realize that in some cases a couple's religious faith complicates the problem. Christian husbands use Scripture to justify their violence.

"Jesus cleansed the temple with a whip. Our bodies are the temples of the Holy Spirit, and when corruption enters that temple it must be driven out. As the head of my wife I am the one to do that for her—with a whip if necessary."

"Ephesians 5 says I am to be the boss, and Jane is to submit to me in all things. It's as simple as that. When she doesn't she has to be disciplined."

Adherence to the doctrine of wifely submission and headship of the authoritarian husband, belief in the permanence and indissolubility of the marriage bond, and belief that on earth we are meant to suffer may, *on the surface*, seem to limit the battered Christian woman's options for dealing with her situation. These are important matters and must be dealt with in a way that neither denies the authority of Scripture nor further victimizes the woman. She needs counseling and support that do not conflict with her spiritual convictions.

What Is the Problem?

Wife abuse is violence by a man against the woman with whom he shares an intimate relationship. It occurs among courting couples and live-in lovers as well as married pairs.

"But what are we actually talking about here?" asked an interested man of a domestic violence counselor. "Do we condemn a guy just for shoving or maybe lightly slapping his wife? Do we jail him on the basis of a single playful swat? I mean, look. Men are naturally, instinctively aggressive."

Aggression may be instinctive to all, but as we mature, each one of us must learn the acceptable ways to show it. An abusive husband has learned he can act aggressively toward his wife to ease tensions building up inside him. Usually he gets away with it. He can be careless with his wife's welfare, and no one rebukes him. He can deliberately treat her harshly and cruelly. He can degrade and demean her, coerce or neglect her. Somewhere he has gotten the idea these selfish patterns of behavior are an acceptable way to express himself.

A woman is considered abused when she is subjected to recurrent forceful physical or psychological attacks. Injuries from physical abuse may be as mild as bruises and cuts, or as serious and potentially lethal as broken bones and teeth, ruptured organs, miscarried pregnancies, and bullet or stab wounds. An abusive husband may push, shove, slap, bite, kick, choke, hit, punch, throw objects at, rape, or force sadistic sexual acts upon his wife. He may threaten her with a weapon, confine her against her will, isolate her from her friends, lock her into or out of the house, or destroy her personal property.

"He wanted me home. I had been at Mom's all day looking after her because she had the flu. He came over after work, grabbed me by the arm, and physically dragged me out. When we got home he locked me in and pulled some wires loose in my car so it wouldn't start."

"I was pregnant and not feeling well at all. Ray got angry because I bought TV dinners for supper. He kicked out a pane of glass in the kitchen window and threw the dinners outside. Then he took a piece of glass and threatened to cut my throat if I ever tried to serve them again."

"He said I was dressed like a tramp so I should be treated like one. He tore off my clothes and beat me with his fists. Then he raped me."

Nonphysical forms of abuse, known as psychological, emotional, and verbal abuse, may accompany physical battering or occur on their own. Women don't have to be beaten to be abused. At the core of nonphysical abuse are the same power and control issues at stake in physically abusive relationships. Here, however, the weapons are words, moods, and mind games.

When a husband employs nonphysical abuse tactics only, his wife may not recognize that she is in fact a victim of abuse. "I'm calling to see if I qualify for your battered women's program," a weary-voiced caller told the intake worker at a shelter. "I don't really think I'm abused. My husband has never actually beaten me up. He has only held a loaded gun to my head and threatened to pull the trigger."

The nonphysically abused woman knows her marriage is in trouble, but her mate's ability to distort reality and intimidate her confuse her as to the true nature of the problem. She often describes her husband as lovable yet volatile, a man who switches instantly from charming to cruel and who, while he can be romantic and exciting, also displays a viciousness and complete lack of sensitivity to the pain and anguish he causes. Thus, she is kept off balance, unable to predict or understand his changes from prince to dragon, and unsure in any particular situation how he will treat her.

Nonphysical abuse is not a matter of mere thoughtlessness or insensitivity or an occasional show of bad temper. It is rather the systematic overpowering of one mate by the other. There are deliberate attempts to manipulate and misrepresent reality. The abuser trivializes events and conveniently forgets what suits him. His victim may be bewildered and confused to the point of doubting her sanity.

"He agreed I could take a night school course and then pretended he'd never said any such thing. He locked me in the bedroom closet for three hours and then said it was a joke."

The abuser makes his partner responsible for all that happens in his world and blames her for all misfortune. Even his most outrageous behavior is her fault.

"How could you go out and get yourself pregnant? You can't even look after me properly. What makes you think you could be a fit mother?"

"If you hadn't made me so angry, I wouldn't have gotten that speeding ticket."

He calls her names, criticizes, insults, ignores, and ridicules her. He humiliates her in public or in private, shows scorn for her opinions and talents, and insists she give up things important to her, such as school, job, community, and church activities.

"He says my business successes are just dumb luck, calls my boutique 'that two-bit shop,' and my friends lesbians and bitches."

"At a party last week, he told everyone I was so fat I jiggle like jello all over when I walk. 'You should see her naked, you'd die laughing.' he said. Then he pointed out how I was blushing."

His tight control of financial matters keeps her totally dependent on him. He handles the books, demands a strict accounting of all she spends, and refuses to divulge his earnings or financial assets.

His tight control of her activities and his constant demands turn her into a robot, jumping at his every command. He forces her to perform demeaning acts— licking his shoes, for example. He uses what she has right to—food and sleep, among other things—as special treats and may withhold them without rhyme or reason on a whim, just to cause her distress and demonstrate his control and power over her.

The abuser may demand or withhold sex, use crude and foul language, and blame his partner for affairs and sexual failures. His sexual relationship with her proceeds without the slightest regard for her feelings or wishes.

Another aspect of nonphysical abuse involves the couple's chilren. The abuser may humiliate his mate in front of them, abuse them in front of her, and threaten to hurt or take them away if she does not comply with his demands of her.

"My husband used to tell our daughters, 'Mommy doesn't love you.'"

"He was so jealous of the babies that I could never play with them or read to them without his coming in and interrupting."

Threats are an abuser's tool as well. He controls his partner with messages of what he will or won't do depending on her behavior.

"If you ever leave me, I'll kill myself."

"Don't think I won't kill you," my husband said, then he shot our dog to prove he could kill."[11]

"If you ever leave me, I'll see to it that you lose custody of the kids. I have connections in this town. Besides, what judge in his right mind would believe a disgusting, pathetic slob like you? You make people sick."

The abuser gains control, in part, through intimidation. He intentionally frightens his victim by his actions— toying with weapons, detailing his past experiences with violence, driving recklessly, throwing tantrums, screaming, raging, glowering, fuming, and generally terrorizing the household.

He also gains control through isolation. His jealousy, possessiveness, and suspicious nature prompt him to sever his wife's ties to her family and friends, either directly by refusing her permission to contact or visit them, or indirectly by belittling them, threatening to harm them, or being obnoxious in their presence.

"Neighbors and their kids bug me. Keep them out of my house."

"Your job is to be my wife. If you're doing that properly, you won't have time to horse around entertaining your parents."

Narrowing her world effectively reduces her ability to view her situation realistically. She has no other relationship with which to compare her own and no one to turn to for affirmation of her good qualities.

Many women feel that their situation is either normal ("That's how married life is, and we have to endure it.") or unique ("Everyone else I know has a happy marriage. Why is mine so bad?"). In the one case, the woman resigns herself to living out what she considers to be the fate of all women, what she saw her mother bear in her own marriage ("Men are brutes. We must endure if we want the security of marriage"). In the other case, pride keeps her from telling anyone how bad things are. It would reflect badly on her, and no one would believe it anyway.

Beth lived with her abusive husband George for more than twenty years before she providentially heard her situation described by a domestic violence counselor on a radio talk show. Until that day she would never have labeled herself abused.

There is something of a stigma attached to being a battered woman. The term seems to imply a bedraggled, harried woman married to a raving, drunken ruffian. An admission of abuse is the end of a wife's fantasy of wedded bliss. It forces her to abandon her pretense of happiness and much of her hope for a better tomorrow.

This stigma, coupled with the victims' ignorance concerning any alternative to their present lifestyle, keeps many from reporting their plight to the authorities. Cultural acceptance of violence between mates and the attitude of law enforcement officials that domestic squabbles should not end in arrest also conspire to keep the battered woman trapped and helpless.

What Is the Cycle of Abusive Behavior?

The abused woman is trapped, too, by the pattern of the violence—how and when it occurs. Researchers, most notably Lenore Walker, have seen in the abusive relationship a three-phase cycle that repeats itself within each family unit.[12] Marital violence is not random and may be predictable in some ways. The length of each phase of the cycle, the events precipitating each phase, and the intensity of each phase may vary from couple to couple, but the order in which the phases occur is apparently a common factor.

First comes the tension-building phase, characterized by the increasing stress both husband and wife experience. Things in Tom's life go wrong and he gets upset. He has a bad day at work, a headache, an unsatisfactory golf score. He comes home irritable, spoiling for a fight. Before long he is screaming at Connie, "You fool, can't you see I don't want my dinner yet? I'm watching the news." Insults may be accompanied by a small amount of physical aggression—a slap or a push.

Connie responds to Tom's anger by trying extra hard to please him. She accepts the blame for his bad temper. "If I could just learn not to bother him when he's tired, everything would be okay." She humbly receives the insults and the slaps. She assures herself that she can control Tom's wrath and keep him from exploding further by being a better wife. She takes care to do whatever he asks; she is compliant and supportive; she cooks his favorite dinner; she caters to him in every way, attempting to keep him satisfied. Tom simmers down and accepts Connie's apologies and submissive behavior. The incident is over. Tom is mollified.

Coaxing and appeasing get Connie through several more minor episodes, and she has a fleeting sensation of being in control for a few days or weeks. However, Tom's behavior worsens, and Connie can no longer placate him. Connie knows what will eventually happen. Her fearful attempts to maintain peace at any price cause her to withdraw from him, anxious not to disturb his tentative self-control. She becomes increasingly afraid to interact with him at all because she never knows what will set him off.

But Tom sees her withdrawal as rejection, and that increases his stress. He cannot bear the thought that she might leave him. He needs to reassure himself that he has her captive, so the more she pulls away, the more he tightens his grip on her. Each little crisis is worse than the last.

Battered women can hardly bear the mental torture of this first phase. They say it is harder to bear than any physical pain. They also recognize they are moving inexorably toward a terrible confrontation, but they don't know when it will happen or what specific incident will be the precipitating one.

The agony has prompted some desperate women to try to arrange to have the explosion occur at a time and place offering them the most advantages. They send the children to spend the night at Grandma's and then provoke an argument to "get it over with." If they can pick the place and time of the assault, they feel less helpless. They don't do this out of any masochistic enjoyment of being beaten. They do it because they can no longer bear the anguish and the suspense of everyday life. They know that a beating will drain away the terrible tension and leave their family life peaceful, at least temporarily. They need an end to the torment.

"What was my reward? A few days, sometimes even weeks with a kind, considerate husband."

Phase two is the explosion. It is the shortest of the three phases, usually lasting no more than twenty-four or at the most forty-eight hours. Anything may precipitate it. A late dinner, a misplaced comb or an unironed shirt, a remark taken the wrong way, anything. Tom decides he must teach Connie a lesson or punish her for some wrongdoing. He believes he has ample justification for his attack.

Overcome by blind rage, allowing his anger to take control, he lashes out wildly, unwilling to stop until he is exhausted and his pent-up frustration and anger are spent. Connie's pleas for mercy go unheard. As with most abusive husbands, Tom finds it difficult to talk about the specifics of the battering later. He says he cannot remember much about what happened and falls back on the excuse that he couldn't help himself. "She got me so mad I didn't know what I was doing."

Connie, however, remembers every detail of this second phase. She is able years later to describe the punches, kicks, and threats Tom used on her during each assault. She doesn't usually fight back during this phase but rather concentrates on protecting herself and surviving. Women who do fight back may find their husbands enraged even more.

When police intervene during this phase, summoned by Connie if she has the chance or by a witnessing neighbor, they frequently try to defuse the situation by calmly talking to Tom, reasoning with him, walking him around the block, and telling him to take a few deep breaths. This is seldom an adequate response. Phase two is so violent that it is useless to try to reason with Tom or talk him out of his anger. Attempts to do so rarely succeed. When the police leave, the beating often resumes.

Then comes phase three. In some ways phase three is the most gruesome because during this phase Connie receives false hope that things will change, that the nightmare existence she lives is over once and for all. Phase three has been called the "honeymoon" because during this time Connie usually experiences the most tender loving she will ever receive from Tom. The tension gone, he is surprised and chagrined at what he has done. He may apologize in abject humility, promising that he will never repeat such behavior again. He may tell her he loves her and that he'll make it up to her if she will promise not to leave him. Or he may say nothing about the beating but be at his most charming to win back her affection and trust. He may buy her gifts, send her flowers and candy, treat her like a queen. The same overkill present in his anger is present in his love. He may bring her not a dozen roses but ten dozen, not a box of chocolates but a new car.

He will do his best to convince everyone involved of his sincerity. He gets his friends to talk to Connie and reassure her of his good intentions if she seems at all skeptical. They bombard her with glowing character references until she gives in and gives him another chance. She can't help but soften. After all, she badly wants to believe that Tom is the Prince Charming he claims to be. During the "honeymoon" Connie and Tom love each other quite tenderly. Tom's loving behavior assures Connie that he really is changing.

In general, the honeymoon is longer than the explosion but shorter than the tension-building phase. It may, however, gradually dwindle in length and intensity over time until it is practically nonexistent. George apologized to Beth less and less over the years as he became convinced she would never leave him no matter what he did to her.

At some point, during the tranquility of phase three, Tom gets upset about something inconsequential, nothing

53

much, nothing Connie cannot handle with a little extra effort, a little coddling. But with this seemingly insignificant act a new phase one is born, and the cycle starts over.

Outlining this sequence of events often proves helpful to victims of abuse and those who wish to help them. Some battered women are shocked to see whole years of their lives fall smoothly into place within the cycle when it is described. Suddenly they understand that any one battering incident will never be the last and that each apology is merely part of the whole battering relationship. This realization can produce feelings of hopelessness. Things, it appears, will never change. But facing reality has its advantages, too. False hopes are no longer generated only to be dashed. It is possible to make serious plans based on the phase of the cycle victims find themselves in at any particular time.

Knowing the cycle helps the friends of a battered woman know what to expect from her. A woman in phase one will be afraid and worried about her situation. She may feel she is coping or she may have reached the point of feeling helpless. She may think of running away.

A woman who has just come through phase two and is recovering from humiliation and injury will be angry and ready to take some action against her spouse to stop any possible repetition of what she has been through. This is the point at which she may most seriously consider leaving him.

Yet given a couple of days, this same woman, now in phase three, will probably soften her attitude. Her husband is now tenderly solicitous, bringing her love in the form of expensive gifts and promises. Forgiveness and optimism may have replaced her fear and anger.

The relationship between husband and wife in a violent marriage is not static. It gets worse. Newspaper stories dramatically reveal the ultimate outcome of unrestrained abuse. As the husband becomes more sure of his wife's helplessness and her acceptance of his actions, no matter how repugnant, his behavior toward her deteriorates. He is less concerned about restricting his aggression toward her. Phase two blow-ups increase in frequency and severity, and phase three make-ups shorten until they disappear. In many cases the final outcome is death:

4 CHILDREN AMONG 6 KILLED IN GUN SPREE

Dead were Bell's estranged wife, his mother-in-law and his four children. One neighbor . . . said Mrs. Bell had left her husband after being abused.[13]

SHOT HUBBY FIVE TIMES

Houston—Kathleen Sandiford celebrates with her son Charles and her attorney Marion Rosen after being convicted of voluntary manslaughter in the shooting death of her husband, heart surgeon Frank Sandiford. . . . She had testified her husband battered and mentally abused her for years and threatened her life shortly before she shot him five times.[14]

BABY FIGHTS FOR LIFE AFTER BEING BORN FOLLOWING MOTHER'S SHOOTING DEATH

Baltimore—UPI—Doctors Tuesday fought to save the life of a premature baby delvs7y Caesarean section nine minutes after his mother died of gunshot wounds inflicted by his father.[15]

WOMAN'S STABBING RULED MURDER BY CORONER'S JURY

Albert Alaway has admitted stabbing his girlfriend, Virginia Payton, after an argument about his clothing.[16]

DOES OUR CULTURE CONTRIBUTE TO ABUSIVE BEHAVIOR?

We live in a violent society. Not only is aggression in males tolerated, it is also sometimes glorified. Our heroes are tough, forceful men who by means of awesome strength (Superman, Mr. T) or the use of futuristic weapons (James Bond) reduce their opponents to quivering, pleading shadows of their former selves. We vicariously enjoy the feeling of superiority that comes from a magic suit of clothes, expertise in the martial arts, or an alliance with an alien. Anything that allows us to prevail over others is highly prized. Marlon Brando, Humphrey Bogart, Charles Bronson, Clint Eastwood, John Wayne—they have played harsh and violent men, and we love them for it.

Such an "ideal" man takes what he wants and is admired for his toughness and strength. He is silent, unemotional, and doesn't tell his "girl" he loves her, but he shows his affection by jealously protecting and possessing her. Sometimes he treats her like a child rather than a fellow adult.

In the 1964 film *Charade*, for example, Cary Grant fell for lovely Audrey Hepburn but found she had an independent spirit and did not always do as she was told. "What you need," he told her in the tone of an exasperated parent, "is a good spanking." [17]

It is sad that we so readily accept abuse as appropriate behavior from people who love each other. We romanticize the domination of women and call it natural for the male to control the female with violence. "A spaniel, a woman, and a hickory tree, the more ye beat them, the better they be," says an old English proverb.

Lucille Ball and Desi Arnaz portrayed a happy young couple in their long-running TV sitcom of the 1950s, "I Love Lucy." But their sunny, funny relationship was *full* of mild abuse. Weekly episodes frequently showed a misbehaving Lucy, cringing in front of Ricky who was shouting Spanish invectives at her. Her arms up to protect her face she would squeal, "Now, Ricky, I can explain!" while audiences roared their approval and sided with Ricky.

Lucy Ricardo accepted the fact that if she was "bad" it was Ricky's prerogative to punish her. One week she overspent her budget and was short of cash. Her friend Ethel suggested, "Why don't you ask Ricky for the money?"

"Because I don't look good in black and blue," Lucy wailed in reply.

Sometimes "for her own good" Lucy got spanked while the TV viewers cheered Ricky on—she always had it coming, didn't she? But, we were reminded at the end of the show, Lucy and Ricky really did love each other very dearly.

Ralph Kramden from "The Honeymooners," played by Jackie Gleason, also made marital violence seem amusing. Was there ever an episode in which he did not in exasperation shake his fist at his wife Alice, threatening to send her "to the moon"?

The message that husbands are provoked beyond endurance by their wives and are entirely justified in controlling them by brute force is not limited to adult entertainment. During an afternoon TV cartoon fest broadcast recently in the Midwest, Woody Woodpecker, dressed as a cave man, club in hand, dragged his "woman" by the hair into his den. Bugs Bunny, doing a Groucho Marx imitation, carrot substituted for cigar, asked a flustered Elmer Fudd, "Have you stopped beating your wife?"

Are Our Adolescents Learning Abusive Behavior?

During adolescence, the messages children have absorbed about the relationship between men and women surface as their own, notably in their music. "Johnny Get Angry," for example, recorded by Joanie Sommers in 1962, tells the story of an adolescent girl who is disappointed by her boyfriend's lack of manliness. It seems he just doesn't measure up. She tells him that if he wants her to look up to him, he will have to show her who's boss. What she wants is a "cave man," someone who, as the title suggests, will "get angry" and scold her when she deserves it. "Johnny," she pleads, "show me that you care, really care, for me."[18] This girl must feel dominated to feel loved. The implication is unless he is possessive, jealous, and rough, how will she ever be sure Johnny loves her?

It may occur to some to point out that many of these

last examples are more than twenty years old. But are such ideas out-of-date? Certainly our liberation mentality has changed our thinking on these matters. Surely we no longer consider brutality toward women or domination of women acceptable.

Regrettably this is not so, says Gene Siskel, *Chicago Tribune* movie critic, commenting on recent films made for teen-age audiences. The female is still considered property of the male. "The dominant images of women in movies today are of . . . women being slashed, knifed, or dancing naked for men's amusement. . . . The teenage girls in today's movies . . . rarely act with intelligence. Nor do they act with initiative."[19]

Edward Donnerstein, professor of communications at the University of Wisconsin, Madison, believes today's teen-age films depict and sustain the standard attitudes toward women held by young men. They see women as possessions to be owned, ordered about, and controlled. "The constant bombardment of women strictly as objects is *definitely* going to maintain and *strongly* reinforce some of those very typical adolescent attitudes in men."[20]

Statistics from studies at several university campuses around the country show that abuse is found and accepted even in dating relationships.[21] At St. John's University in Minnesota, James Makepeace, a professor of sociology, conducted a survey of student behavior in 1979. Twenty-one percent of the responding students reported being abused in a premarital relationship. At Oregon State University, Rodney M. Cate of the university's family life development staff found that nearly twenty-five percent of his study sample were experiencing this problem before marriage.

In 1980 Mary Riege, a sociologist at Arizona State University, discovered a staggering sixty percent of surveyed students were involved either as abusers or as victims in abusive relationships. And, she noted, these were serious pairings. In fact, abuse is most likely to occur in committed rather than casual relationships. As in Joanie

Sommers's song of twenty years ago, violence is still thought to indicate love.

Is Wife Abuse Really a New Problem?

The publicity that spouse abuse has received lately makes it appear its occurrence is on the rise. Besides books and articles that are now being published, battering is also depicted in prime time TV shows and in newspaper comic strips.[22] It has become fashionable for famous abusers to admit their problem to the press. British actor Oliver Reed, for instance, boasted of being an abuser in a 1976 magazine interview.[23] The April 1983 issue of *People* featured a cover photograph of actor David Soul with this caption: "The Crime of David Soul—Charged with wife abuse he confronts the turmoil in his violent marriage."

However, the truth is that a centuries-old cover-up is disintegrating, and this heretofore "private" crime is coming out into the open at last. The incidence is not increasing—our awareness is. A brief foray into the past helps make the point that wife abuse is a matter of historical record.

The earliest chronicles of man's existence note the superior position granted husbands over their wives. Women in ancient patriarchal societies were considered the property of their husbands, fathers, or other male kin, and as such were "collectable." Men who could afford them had hundreds of wives. These women had few, if any, rights, and many restrictions were placed on them. Even the Hebrew nation living under the authority of God had customs based on the inferiority of women. Women, for instance, could not testify in a court of law because they were considered unreliable witnesses. The daily prayer of the orthodox Jewish male intoned: "Blessed art Thou, O Lord, our God, King of the universe, who hast not made me a heathen, a slave, or a woman."

Jesus' earthly life substantially changed all that for many women. He was a revolutionary force in the world and quietly demonstrated a respect for women, which had a profound effect on His followers. He taught women openly, visited them in their homes, numbered them among His disciples, healed and vindicated them in front of others. Later the apostles followed in His footsteps by welcoming women as co-workers in preaching the gospel around the world. The apostle Paul repudiated the traditional Jewish prayer with these statements from his letter to the Galatian churches: "For as many of you as were baptized into Christ have put on Christ. There is neither Jew nor Greek, there is neither slave nor free, there is neither male nor female; for you are all one in Christ Jesus" (Gal. 3:27-28).

Unfortunately, but not unexpectedly, this new attitude toward women did not last. Nor did the idea of the superior position of men, taken from Scripture, inspire tender protection or a generous caring attitude on the part of husbands. Instead it confirmed the male conviction that the most basic courtesy and consideration given to others in general need not be practiced toward wives. The gentlemanly and noble spirit of behaving well toward those entrusted to one's care did not apply to the treatment of women. They were merely objects to be used as a man might wish.

Early in the twelfth century a scholar named Gratian wrote a book of theology that included the explanation for a husband's position of authority over his wife. Since Eve beguiled Adam, his theory went, it was only right that every woman from then on should be under her husband's direction. Thus no woman would ever have the opportunity to mislead a man again.[24]

Traditions that solidly fixed the superior position of men over women expanded to include the belief that men also had the right to beat their wives. This right was considered essential and benevolent in that it helped keep women well behaved and virtuous.

Throughout the Middle Ages brutality was rampant, and cruelty to wives was actually institutionalized—condoned and encouraged by the church. Women were burned at the stake for scolding, nagging, or making threats against their husbands—even for miscarrying a pregnancy when the miscarriage was the result of assault by the husband.[25] The church was a strong legal force and controlled the civil courts. It misused Scripture and gave its ecclesiastical blessing to domestic violence.

In sixteenth-century Russia the state church issued an ordinance itemizing the most effective means a husband might use to punish his wife. He was even allowed to kill her if the act was a disciplinary measure.[26]

Slowly, with the passing of many years, restrictions were added to the "chastisement" laws in most countries. Although British common law, so called for being based on what the community deemed correct, gave husbands the explicit right to punish their wives, its "Rule of Thumb" restrained them from using a rod for the beating any larger in diameter than their thumb. Still, acts of brutality that would have been considered assault if committed by a stranger were rendered innocent when committed by a husband.

The United States' legal system evolved out of the British model. The law allowed a woman to be beaten for correctional purposes. Wife assault was regulated, not condemned or criminalized. Abuse was accepted, even expected husbandly behavior. Marital violence was a man's privilege, and the rationalization persisted that the beatings were actually for the wife's benefit—to make her a better person. As late as 1824, Mississippi law held that a husband had the right to chastise his wife moderately in emergency situations.

Although wife beating came to be seen as less and less appropriate, the courts were reluctant to become involved in marital violence cases. It was considered preferable to let the mates work things out themselves in the privacy of their own home.

After the Civil War, court decisions began to more stringently limit the husband's prerogative to punish his wife. Finally, in 1871, an Alabama court set a precedent by ruling that men no longer held any right to injure or mistreat their wives. The decision stated that "the privilege, ancient though it may be, to beat her with a stick, to pull her hair, choke her, spit in her face or kick her about the floor, or to inflict upon her other like indignities, is not now acknowledged by our law."[27]

It is now against the law in every state for a husband to abuse his wife physically, to confine her, or to compel her obedience by force. Even so, the tacit acceptance of the practice and the covering up of the crime have been formidable barriers to dealing with it. Enforcing laws prohibiting spouse battering is not easy. The conspiracy of silence by those directly involved, and the minimizing and trivializing of it by law enforcement officials and counselors, only serve to perpetuate this age-old tragedy.

In 1962 a California woman who had been beaten by her husband was denied a chance to present her case to the state supreme court because bringing such a case to trial would "destroy the peace and harmony of the home, and thus would be contrary to the policy of the law."[28] It is interesting to note the judge felt the beating itself did not disrupt the peace and harmony of the home, but its public disclosure would.

More than twenty years later, our society is proving slow at ending the suffering of battered women. The recent publicity the issue has received is putting pressure on authorities at every level to consider wife abuse unacceptable and to take seriously the protection of the victim and the prosecution of the abuser. But there is still a long way to go.

In 1983 a district court judge in Denver came under fire for a decision he handed down in a murder trial. He had sentenced a forty-seven-year-old man to two years' probation and weekends in jail for killing his wife. Judge Alvin Lichtenstein explained the light sentence was based on the fact the man's wife had left him abruptly and this highly provocative act would have "excited an irresistible passion . . . in any reasonable person."[29] Governor Richard Lamm called the sentence outrageous. An incensed citizen pointed out in a subsequent newspaper story that the murderer would have received a stiffer sentence for shooting an eagle—or even a neighbor's dog. Public outcry had an effect, but only a paltry one.

The judge lengthened the sentence to four years' probation.

3

Who Are the Participants in Wife Abuse?

For it is not an enemy who reproaches me;
Then I could bear it.
Nor is it one who hates me who has magnified
   himself against me;
Then I could hide from him.
But it was you, a man my equal,
My companion and my acquaintance.
We took sweet counsel together,
And walked to the house of God in the throng
(Ps. 55:12–14).

WHO IS THE ABUSER?

Who is the man who abuses his wife? He may be anyone. The psalmist's chagrin, disbelief, and sense of betrayal in Psalm 55 are echoed by battered women everywhere who discover that the considerate and tender men who lovingly courted them have turned into brutes and bullies. Not one of these women set out to marry a wife beater.

It has been discovered in compiling a profile of the abuser that he is indigenous to all populations, races, classes, religions, age groups, educational levels, and cultures. In most respects he is not substantially different from his nonviolent fellows. He is a businessman, a teacher, a factory worker, a policeman, a lawyer, a professional athlete, a shoe repairman, a Ph.D., a construction worker, a florist, a dentist, a truck driver, a clergyman, a radio announcer, a Hollywood celebrity, a physician, an unemployed laborer, or a member of the armed forces.[1]

At one time the general feeling about him was that he was mentally ill. Now it is believed that while there are a few cases of severe mental illness among batterers, battering is more of an emotional disturbance. The incidence of wife abuse is far too pandemic to be the work of a few psychotics.

Due to a complex combination of psychological, sociological, and cultural factors, some men, needing to feel in control, choose violence as the quickest and most efficient way to obtain it. The usual excuse given is "to make my wife behave; to teach her a lesson."

He is not altogether an unlovable tyrant. He may be an affectionate father and a respected member of the community, good at his job and active in service organizations. One of his most attractive qualities may be that he seems very much in control and capable of handling everything.

This being the case, onlookers cannot help wondering what is inside him that allows him to be so destructive toward the one person in his life he should cherish above all others. While each abusive husband is different from the rest, most do have some of the following characteristics in common.

Abusers have experienced violence as children.

Suzanne Steinmetz studied violence in families and discovered that children imitate their parents' fighting techniques when fighting among themselves. If they see slapping, they slap each other. If they hear name calling, they use the same epithets on their siblings. When they grow up and marry, they continue to use those same patterns of behavior with their spouses and their own children.[2] Men who have grown up watching their parents engage in physical violence, therefore, are the ones most likely to physically abuse their own mates.

Many abusive men were either victims themselves or witnessed violence between their parents. The horror and helplessness they felt in those experiences affect them all their lives. They understand how it feels to be the victim. As adults they crave the protection and nurturing they missed as children, but they have also learned that the strongest member of the family gets to decide what the others will do.

Abusers are dissatisfied with themselves.

Childhood mistreatment or rejection may be responsible for giving an abuser a very unfavorable self-image. Regardless of his occupation or status in the community, he feels he doesn't measure up to society's ideal. His poor self-image causes him much frustration. He feels weak and resorts to violence to assure himself that he really is strong.

One way to deny his own weakness is to emphasize the weakness of another, notably his wife.

"She's so stupid she can't write a check or change a light bulb."

He isolates himself from others so they will not see how inadequate he is. The abuser is often a man with a history of being a loner. Like Beth's George, he may have many friendships, but they are superficial. In public he seems congenial and compliant, but he always keeps his distance. He may be able to assist others, but he cannot ask for help himself. Because he is so unhappy with himself, he dare not reveal the real man he is to anyone— even to his wife. In fact, his fear of intimacy is most obvious at home, where he cannot allow himself to show tenderness, uncertainty, or sorrow but must always demonstrate strength, control, and masculine power.

Abusers are dependent.

It might seem strange that a man who utterly controls and dominates his wife is also completely dependent on her, but this is the case. The abuser feels that his wife is the only one he is really close to. He believes that he absolutely cannot live without her. He values her above all else, not for who she is but for what she contributes to his self-esteem. "She's my woman—all mine."

He cannot bear the thought that he might lose her undivided attention. Her slightest move toward any kind of independence, therefore, can bring on violence. Feeling undeserving of her love, he must go to great lengths to keep her. Because all other men, being more desirable than he, are potential thieves ready to seduce her and carry her away, he must monitor all her activities, isolate her from her friends, and use whatever means are necessary to control her.

If she should leave, he will do everything he can to get her to return. He will promise to reform, beg and cry on his knees, loudly threaten suicide, craftily hint at revenge, or claim a religious conversion. He must get her back at any cost.

Abusers feel hostility toward women.

Abusers seem to share a common hatred for women. They hold fast the stereotypical belief in the inferiority of the female and believe wives must be kept "in line."

"She's your woman—your property. What you do with her is your own business and nobody else's."

"Are you telling me I don't have a right to tell my wife what to do? She's mine, isn't she?"

He may bluntly and proudly label himself a male chauvinist, and typically he holds rigid traditional views of marriage and marital roles. He believes the male role *demands* the use of force and bravado as proof of one's superior masculinity.

"She gets a bit too uppity, a bit too sure of herself, and I knock her around a little. Nothing to really hurt her, you know, I've just got to get her kind of scared and helpless—under my control."

Above all, this man needs to feel "in charge." He cannot tolerate wifely autonomy. For instance, his wife must not work outside the home. If she does, she must turn over her earnings to him. She must not have ties in the community—membership in clubs or organizations, and responsibilities that do not include him—for such things take her out from under his control.

Abusers deny they are abusive.

It is very painful for an abusive husband to recognize and admit his cruelty. The woman toward whom he is violent is the one with whom he is most intimately connected. He deals with his guilt by minimizing or even denying his violent behavior. "I pushed her around a little," he might admit, but he downplays, to himself and to others, the real seriousness and destructiveness of his actions. At times he may flatly refuse to acknowledge his behavior. "I didn't hurt her. I would never hurt her!"

Even if he is arrested he will not concede that he has done wrong. "There's nothing the matter with me," he will adamantly maintain.

He staunchly claims he has a right to act in this way, but his attempts to cover up his behavior demonstrate that he knows he is wrong. He only hits his wife when no one else is around. He threatens her with further violence should she tell anyone what he has done to her. He lies to his friends, relatives, and on occasion to medical personnel about the source of his wife's injuries. He holds her in contempt for allowing him to get away with it.

Abusers blame others.

The abuser often attributes his successes and his failures to outside forces. He wins the company tennis tournament not because he played well, but because he was wearing his lucky shirt. His colleague gets the promotion *he* wanted only because of favoritism on the boss's part. The problems he faces, too, are directly the fault of someone else. He is late for work because his wife doesn't lay out the right clothes for him. The blame for his violence is also placed elsewhere. "You *force* me to hurt you," he tells his wife.

The abuser uses any and all excuses to keep from taking responsibility for his actions. "I was so drunk I didn't know what I was doing." Thus, the pattern of blaming others persists even in the face of logical argument to the contrary.

Abusers are angry.

The abuser is likely to be a man who is out of touch with his emotions. He tends to express feelings of anxiety, fear, sorrow, guilt, or helplessness as anger. If someone in his family is seriously ill, he experiences fury, not anguish. If a situation frightens him, he feels rage, not terror. He is either humming along placidly or he is irate. Any emotional reaction he has can trigger violence. Battered wives say they are never sure what will precipitate an attack.

"There was a rumor that his plant was going to shut down production right after the holidays. The day he heard it, my Jack just went wild. He busted about every stick of furniture in the place, some of it over my head," reported one battered wife.

Abusers are childish.

An abusive husband is frequently an immature man, easily bored and restless, a childish, self-centered and narcissistic man who needs lots of attention.

"John is like a little boy who wants to be grown up. It's like he's playing at being an adult, and everyone else *has* to go along with him or he'll throw a tantrum."

He often acts without thinking, impulsively changing jobs or quitting, selling his house and moving to another city on a whim, buying a yacht or investing in gold at a moment's notice. He makes important decisions without prior consideration of the ramifications and with a naive disregard for the consequences.

Abusers cannot tolerate stress.

The batterer is unable to cope with stress or handle frustration in a nonaggressive way. No matter what produces the tension—his wife's pregnancy, a disobedient child, pressure from work, feelings of failure—he lashes out to relieve it. In general, people tend to take out their frustrations on those closest to them, and the abusive husband is no exception. When he feels he cannot cope with the world, his wife is the logical one to bear the brunt of his agitation. She may try her best to keep him soothed, calm, and relaxed, but since it is impossible to provide a totally stress-free environment for anyone, she faces an impossible task.

Abusers lack good communication skills.

The batterer also lacks the ability to communicate well verbally. He doesn't know how to talk things over and would never share his inner thoughts or private self with anyone. This closed, shut-off facade fosters misunderstandings between him and those close to him. His wife feels left out, misinterprets his quietness as rejection, and draws erroneous conclusions from the silence.

As she tries to draw him out, he feels increasingly uncomfortable. Often marital arguments start this way and end up a springboard to physical violence. Feeling inarticulate and inadequate to express himself well, the husband may decide to settle matters with his fists. Physical power, he discovers, ends arguments and resolves differences quite nicely in his favor. Assaults on wives frequently follow verbal arguments where the husband feels ineffective. The more often disagreements turn to assaults, the easier the transition becomes.

Abusers frequently have alcohol and drug related problems.

In the past, it was felt that drinking was the cause of the abusive man's violence. Many still believe that substance abuse accounts for 70 to 80 percent of wife abuse cases.[3] Others contend that while there is a significant incidence of alcohol use among abusers, it is no higher than in the general population.[4] They feel that substance abuse and violence are two separate overlapping problems affecting our society today.

Heavy drinking, while it certainly contributes to wife abuse, is probably not actually causative, but rather tends to trigger violence. Drinking lowers inhibitions and impairs judgment. The man who drinks is out of control. Rage increases with drinking, and the ability to contain the rage is lost. In fact, drinking provides a plausible excuse for the batterer. "I was not myself. I was drunk. I didn't know what I was doing." Some men drink in order to be able to disclaim responsibility for their abusive actions later. Drunkenness supplies a socially acceptable reason for the violence.

Richard Gelles, assistant professor of sociology at the University of Rhode Island, explains, "Having become drunk and then violent the individual may deny what occurred ['I don't remember, I was drunk'], or plead for forgiveness ['I didn't know what I was doing']. In both cases he can shift the blame for violence from himself to the effects of alcohol."[5] In this way he can indulge in prohibited activities without risking much censure or punishment.

Even the victims of abuse cling to the fact that their husbands only hurt them when they are drunk. "He'd never treat me this way if he could help it," they say. "But when he's drinking he doesn't know what he's doing." Attributing abuse to the alcohol makes it easier to forgive the man.

But when these men are sent through detoxification programs and get their drinking problems under control, they often still beat their wives. Violence does not automatically stop when the husband is sober.

Addiction to drugs, particularly cocaine, is another trigger for battering behavior. Cocaine use has increased dramatically in this country over the past two years—up from 15 to 20 million users.[6] Although not everyone who uses cocaine becomes violent, the drug is a stimulant and will heighten the excitement and anger of someone who is already violent. Shelters across the country are admitting ever larger numbers of women who have been battered by cocaine-using mates.

Unfortunately, drug addiction, too, tends to provide a handy excuse. "Oh, well, what else could you expect? He's a drug addict. Poor guy."

Whether it is alcohol or drug use that is the abuser's problem, his wife must not allow herself to excuse his behavior on that basis. Drunk or high on drugs, he is nevertheless still responsible for his actions.

HOW TO SPOT THE ABUSER

A man may turn abusive after marriage when tender courtship and chivalry are no longer necessary to maintain his hold on his chosen woman, but some men do not wait for a marriage license to begin acting aggressively. Premarital abuse is not uncommon. Women who are victims of such abuse frequently cling to the hope that in marriage their husbands will feel secure, and the abuse will cease.

But this does not happen. Abuse in courtship presages a married life filled with misery. Women should be aware of danger signals that portend a violent spouse. A woman should call an immediate halt to any relationship with a man who:

- is intensely, albeit flatteringly, jealous—perhaps even jealous of her father and brother.

- smothers her, wants her all to himself, and requires her to give up her other friendships.

- needs to possess and control her, to tell her what to do, what to wear, where to go, and when to go there.

- experiences fits of uncontrolled anger at inanimate objects or circumstances and often breaks things while in this mood.

- acts aggressively toward the helpless and defenseless—children and pets, for instance.

- routinely insults or belittles her or is in any way physically violent toward her, shoving, slapping, pushing, biting, or hurting her in any way.

HOW TO SPOT THE VICTIM

On the surface the abused wife may be the epitome of society's traditional values. She is submissive, strong in her religious faith, a woman who follows where her husband leads. Her marriage is the most important thing in her life, and she is completely devoted to her home and family. She grew up believing that once she found her man, life would be beautiful forever. She is supposed to make him happy; *she* must make the marriage work. The abused wife may gladly put her husband first in everything.

She may share the view of many women, particularly Christian women, that the female is innately inferior to the male. Her man is her superior, and she looks down on all women, herself included, as mere subordinates.

Wives who get beaten are generally not liberated, headstrong women. They have not, as some would suggest, usurped their husbands' authority as head of the house and taken over his divinely appointed place of leadership. On the contrary, they love their husbands, stick up for them, and protect them from the disapproval of outsiders. They are the first ones to list their mates' good qualities to others, and until they get really desperate they minimize violence done to them.

Abused women seem to fall into two broad categories.[7] First, there are women from predominantly conservative, traditional backgrounds. These women have been raised in loving homes by parents who have brought them up gently, without physical punishment. The families profess a religious faith, do not accept or condone divorce, and want their daughters' husbands to be men who will look after them well.

These women react to their abuse with shock and embarrassment, but the family stigma concerning broken marriages makes it impossible for them to get out of their predicament. These women also feel their families would not believe or understand that their lives are so miserable.

Second, there is a smaller group of women from violent homes for whom marriage is a chance to escape a domineering, coercive father. But in marrying an abuser they find they have merely traded one tyrant for another. Since they have grown up with violence, they expect and accept it as normal. Witnessing parental violence may have instilled in them a subliminal approval of it. Many of them feel confident at first that they will be able to endure or overcome even though their mothers could not. They, too, strongly cling to traditional sex role standards. Men must be manly and rough, women tender and submissive.

In both groups of women the idea persists that marriage gives life meaning and is responsible for one's status. They feel they have no value as individuals apart from their men. They have learned from childhood that a women is not complete without a husband.

Entering a relationship with a batterer could happen to any woman. She is courted with gentleness and gallantry, perhaps flattered by possessiveness and jealousy, and she looks forward to a life warmed and sustained by mutual tenderness and devotion. When violence first rears its head, she reacts with shock and disbelief. Her response to the assault is most likely to be cowering passivity rather than retaliation or revenge.

She believes her husband's apologies because she loves him and wants everything to be all right. Of course everything is not all right. She tries to cover up the abuse as long as she can, wanting to continue to convince the world that she is indeed living happily ever after. Outward appearances must be maintained at all costs.

Having been taught from childhood that a husband makes one fulfilled and happy, she dare not admit her plight. If she does, she is forced to blame herself for her predicament. "What did I do wrong?" After some introspection she may think of ways to make everything better. She sets a new course for herself, confident that it will all work out somehow. She may fool herself for years by denying or minimizing the violence and heaping the blame on herself.

Then one day she can deny it no longer. Overwhelmed by her husband's cruelty, certain that she cannot endure it one more day, she seeks help, first from her family ("You made your bed, now lie in it. A good woman can change a man") and then from her friends ("What did you do to make him so angry?"). She may also get advice from her pastor ("Pray for strength to bear the cross God has given you"), her doctor ("Take these pills and see if that doesn't calm you down"), the police ("You two kiss and make up. This is something you have to work out between yourselves"), and a marriage counselor ("We can't help you unless both you and your husband agree to be seen together"). If all these fail her, she succumbs to despair. She is the complete victim.

She lives in terror, having learned that she cannot help herself or expect help from others. Her self-confidence drains away as she continues to listen to her husband's harangues about her worthlessness and inadequacy. She becomes resigned, incapable of independent thinking, a collaborator in her own ruin. She withdraws from everyone and hates herself more and more. She no longer thinks about getting help. She has given up.

Our society rates love very highly. A woman must love and be loved by a man in order to be a good person. Love can change a beast or a frog into a prince. Without love there is nothing to live for; a woman cannot survive without it. So the battered woman must hang on to the idea that she loves her mate. She must continue to believe her love for him will transform her tormentor into her prince. She cannot allow herself to admit being angry with him, for if she does, her whole world crumbles. She will grasp at straws to make sense out of her chaotic life.

"It took some thinking, but I finally figured out what I have been doing wrong. I haven't been giving him enough love. Now that I know what to do, he'll never have to hurt me again."

"I actually thought if I learned to keep house like his mother, and cook like a French chef, everything would fall into place and run smoothly. I kept on believing it through seven years of assaults."

"SHE GOT WHAT SHE DESERVED!"

A popular myth says that wives provoke their beatings by pushing their husbands too far. Battered women are blamed for the beatings they receive ("The poor guy probably stood it as long as he could") and for not ending them ("If she would just quit nagging him, none of this would happen"). If they leave, they are blamed for the consequences that accrue to their husbands ("She had him arrested, and he lost his job because of it") and to the family ("She walked out on him and broke up their home"). They are blamed for *not* seeking help ("She puts up with it so she must be getting something out of it") and for seeking help ("She called the cops on him. Imagine having your own husband arrested. How could she do that?").

Battered women take these accusations to heart. They readily assume the blame, look for the mistakes they made, and attempt to isolate the things they say and do that *make* their husbands hurt them. They feel responsible for the assaults.

"I never seem to be able to say the right thing."

"I know if I get myself on a schedule so that I can keep the house the way he likes it, he'll stop beating me so much. I just can't seem to keep up with the mess he and the four kids make. And that really bugs him."

Of course abused women are not to blame. For one thing, much of the violence they experience could not by any stretch of the imagination be their fault. For example, if Rick comes home from the office furious over a criticism from his boss, he bellows at Linda before he has his coat off. Nothing she did caused or could prevent his attack. And Lloyd: he lies awake at night working himself into a frenzy over June's possible unfaithfulness with his partner or a neighbor or the gardener. He wakes her up out of a sound sleep, kicking, punching, and screaming threats at her. Then there is Bill. He beat Sharon one day for leaving too many lights on in the house, and the next day he beat her because the porch light was *not* on when he got home from work.

It must be pointed out, too, the things that provoke an abusive husband to beat his wife are frequently things that would not faze a nonviolent man. His wife may serve a vegetable he is not fond of, cough during a TV show he is watching, or "too cheerfully" greet the mail carrier.

It is impossible for two people to live together as husband and wife without occasional disagreements. The closeness of the relationship guarantees this will be so. Quarrels, however, do not provide sufficient grounds for violence. The question, "What does she do to provoke him?" diverts attention from the real question, "Does a husband ever have the right to abuse his wife?" The answer is clearly no. Blaming women for causing men to batter them condemns the victim of a crime and justifies the criminal. It arbitrarily gives one person permission to injure another and disregards the fact that violence is unacceptable.

A related misconception labels the battered woman masochistic and postulates that she enjoys being beaten, even obtains sexual gratification from it. If this were true, there would be no issue here and no problem to deal with. Each partner would be getting what he or she wanted from the relationship. But women do not want it, enjoy it, or need it. They live with it, tolerate it, endure it, but in great agony. Professionals who work with battered women do not believe these victims cause or want the abuse they receive.

"WHY DOES SHE STAY WITH HIM?"

Perhaps the most frequently asked question on the lips of those who hear about battering for the first time or see the evidence of it on the face of a friend or relative is, "Why would a woman continue to put up with that? Why does she stay?"

Many women, of course, do not stay. Court rosters in most cities are crowded with divorce cases, many of them the result of violence. The number of shelters available across the country to house battered wives is increasing as public awareness of their plight increases. There are now more than twelve hundred, and they are always full, with long waiting lists.[8]

The answer as to why some women stay is so complex it cannot be summed up in a sentence or short paragraph. There are many different reasons, some more concrete and obvious than others.

Religious convictions are cited by a number of battered women. They believe their faith prohibits them from separating from their husbands or seeking divorce. These beliefs are reinforced when they go to clergymen for help with their marital problems. They hear what Beth heard from her pastor, "Don't expect me to tell you it's all right for you to leave George, because I won't."

Some women stay with their mates because they think they have no place to go. "I left home in a panic four times, but always ended up back home with my husband because I had nowhere to go."

Shelters are an answer for some women, but for others no such facility is nearby. Relatives offer hope to some women, but for others parents live too far away or are unsympathetic to their daughter's situation. A battered woman, long isolated from her friends, may no longer have anyone to call on for help in a crisis.

Often economic hardship is the reason a wife does not leave. Many a battered woman is her husband's economic prisoner with little or no access to cash. She is frequently, but not always, an unemployed housewife, unfamiliar with basic budgeting skills and entirely ignorant in matters of loans and credit. Even if she is employed, sometimes as principal breadwinner, her husband looks after the money, and she is kept penniless, which is one of his techniques to ensure his control over her. Should she decide to leave, she must reckon with the fact that in doing so she will in most cases substantially lower her standard of living. Regardless of whether she fears poverty for herself, she may be reluctant to assign this burden to her children.

Children, too, are an important factor. For the most part, battered women are conscientious mothers and want the best for their children. That best includes a home with a father.

"I couldn't raise the kids myself," they say. "It's far too great a responsibility. The kids need their dad, and he loves them. I couldn't separate them from each other."

These women buy into the idea that any father is better than no father, not realizing how damaging continued exposure to parental violence is for their little ones.

Ironically, however, if the children are the reason some women stay with their mates, they may also prove ultimately to be the reason those women leave. Battered women will passively accept aggression directed toward themselves but react like mother bears when their young are attacked.

"One day he slapped Karen the same way he slapped me, and I said to myself, 'All right. Enough is enough. This has got to end.' And I took the girls and left for good."

"My nine-year-old son started imitating his dad's behavior toward his sister and me. It broke my heart and made me realize I had to do something to stop the whole mess."

For some battered women the explanation for why they stay lies not in outward circumstances but deep within themselves. In many cases, an overwhelming, immobilizing fear paralyzes the battered woman much like the headlights of an approaching car catch and hold a rabbit. She knows her husband could kill her. She knows he cannot be stopped. She lives from minute to minute, concentrating on survival. She dare not make plans to escape because if he ever found out, that would enrage him more. An abusive husband cannot stand by and let his wife leave him. She is his scapegoat and his source of stability. "If you ever try to get away from me," he warns her, "I'll find you and kill you."

He may scream it or whisper it, but she knows he is deadly serious. Beth stayed with George for years because of her fear he would kill her if she left. Case records of many agencies confirm these are not idle words.

"I'd rather stay with him than be stalked like an animal for the rest of my life. He'd follow me anywhere just to get revenge."

"It is the most horrible, terrifying feeling to know that someone is hunting you—that any minute you may see his face at your window or find him beside you on the sidewalk. I just can't live with that kind of pressure."

The abused woman fears, too, for the safety of her family or any friends whose lives might be endangered by helping her.

"My mom says to come home and stay with her, but she's so old and frail. Marty would think nothing of killing her, too."

"I tried to leave once. I got as far as my sister's. Then he called and told me, 'Come back to me, Sylvia, or I'll make it very rough on certain people in your family. I'm through playing games.'"

Abusive husbands harass acquaintances, relatives, and co-workers of their wives to force them to return. They even attempt to intimidate shelter counselors.

"We finally had to put Jane at the phone full time just to field the threatening calls we were getting from Kay's husband. He must have called every fifteen to thirty minutes day and night for two weeks—I kid you not—before he wore out," a social worker at one shelter recalls.

Other fears plague the battered woman. As she contemplates the possibility of escape, the fear of loneliness is likely to loom up in her mind and with it fear of taking on total responsibility for her family. It is hard to make plans for a major change in her way of living. Fear of the unknown may seem worse than the terror of her present violent but familiar world.

The battered woman also has strong emotional ties to the man she married, brutal though he may be. When she considers leaving, she remembers their courtship and the good times they have shared. Happy memories crowd into her mind to revive feelings of love she thought were lost forever. His charming "honeymoon" behavior after his violent episodes confuses her and dilutes her resolve to get out.

She has been taught that it is her role to care for her husband. She views his violence as a sign that he is sick and needs her to minister to him. Perhaps a loving, nurturing person by nature, she feels sorry for him, and this emotion is intensified by his family and her friends who may tell her, "Joe has serious problems. You're his only hope. He needs you desperately. Without you he will be destroyed."

She finds it hard to turn a deaf ear to her husband himself, who deluges her with an ocean of pleas and promises. There are apologies ("I'm so sorry. Forgive me, Darling, I'm begging you") and vows ("I swear it will never happen again. I'm going to get some counseling"), glowing testimonies of conversion ("I've found the Lord, Chrissie, really I have"), and concern for her welfare ("You'll never make it without me. Let me take care of you"). Already ambivalent, she is hard-pressed to withstand such appeals to her caring, affectionate spirit.

The abusive husband may repeatedly assure his wife he will change. He sounds sincere, and she wants to believe him. She wants the wonderful future he promises and the fantasy life without struggles and heartaches he describes. Her trust is so strong that it takes years and years of broken vows and false repentances for it to die completely. The longer she stays with her mate, the harder it is to leave.

It is also difficult for a battered woman to walk away from the one who is her security blanket. Emotionally her identity is wrapped up in being dependent on her man. She was never taught to stand on her own two feet or to make it on her own, but to "marry a nice boy and settle down. Let him have a career. You have the children." Years of controlling and coercive behavior from her husband add to her sense of helplessness.

Counselor Lenore Walker describes experiments in which laboratory animals and human volunteers were confined and then exposed to random, painful stimuli over which they had no control and from which they could not escape. Once they realized their behavior had no effect on what happened to them, their motivation to help themselves seemed to die. They ceased trying to get away or gain relief, actually ignoring obvious avenues of escape, even when these were pointed out. When they had learned they were powerless, they stopped struggling and became passive. In much the same way, Walker says, the battered woman learns she can do nothing to save herself from her husband's wrath. Her motivation to solve her problems dissolves. She may become so passive and withdrawn that she can hardly be persuaded to seek relief.[9]

Emotional and financial dependency become more serious hindrances to escape when it is noted that the abused woman is also completely isolated from anyone on whom she might call for assistance. Her husband takes pains to separate her from other women, from her relatives, and from the community in general. Because of this she must rely on him for her every need. Her dependency on him and him alone cuts her off from potential rescuers and valuable allies. Without a source of support, someone to believe in her and encourage her, she may truly be locked into her situation. Thus her isolation increases her fear of leaving. As one battered woman remarked, "I didn't have anyone to turn to anymore. I only felt safe at home even though that's where I got hurt. At least home was familiar territory."

In depriving her of social contacts her husband contributes to her confusion about her situation. He tells her one thing ("It's your own fault you get beaten") and she perceives another ("I did nothing to deserve this"). Without outside corroboration to confirm her point of view, she may begin to think she is insane ("Is everything really my fault? What am I doing wrong? Am I crazy?").

A lack of self-esteem often characterizes the abused woman. "The more he abused me, the less my family thought of me and the less I thought of myself. I became convinced that I wasn't good enough for any man. I felt lucky he would have me, no matter how he abused me."[10]

Self-respect and self-confidence are aspects of the battered woman's personality that are the most seriously damaged by her husband. He pounds it into her that she is inadequate, stupid, and worthless.

She has had no practice taking the initiative or making decisions, and she doubts her ability to do so. A separation from her husband would be impossible and full of responsibilities she knows she could never handle. She tells herself she could not balance a checkbook, deal with a landlord, or raise the children on her own.

Abuse is frequently too horrible and demeaning to be confessed to friends. In covering it up the battered wife can salvage a few shreds of dignity. Shame is a real obstacle preventing her from taking action to help herself. She cannot bear to "air the dirty family linen" before others. Her husband takes advantage of, and gains confidence from, her reticence to speak out. He realizes he is safe from discovery because she won't tell.

In short, without support from others the battered woman is often trapped by her husband, by society, and by herself. It takes a great deal of strength to overcome all the obstacles that stand in the way of her move to safety and a better life.

WHO IS THE FAMILY IN AN ABUSIVE HOME ENVIRONMENT?

Are the Children also Victims?

Child rearing produces stress in all families, violent and nonviolent, and this stress begins with the first pregnancy. Abused women report beatings occur more frequently during their pregnancies than at other times, with a majority of the blows they receive being aimed at their abdomens. It is theorized that expectant fathers may find themselves subject to extra tension during the months preceding the birth of a child. They are faced with new responsibility and added financial burdens. They must cope with changes in daily routines and in the wife's behavior. They may be dealing with the sexual frustration produced by the belief that one should abstain from intercourse until the child is born. The wife's greater defenselessness brings about the urge in some men to hurt her more. An abusive man may also feel a certain jealousy toward this new person who will consume all his wife's attention. Battering during pregnancy may be an attempt at abortion. Miscarriages can and do occur as a result of it.

The presence of infants and toddlers in a family also

tends to create stress. This may be because children of these ages demand a large amount of attention and cannot wait for it, often proclaiming their impatience in loud and irritating ways. An abusive husband wants his wife all to himself. He resents the time the children require and responds badly to their crying and fussing.

Households with adolescents are no less volatile places. When there is a concurrent abusive situation, the presence of teen-agers seems to set off an increase in the number of explosive incidents.

Children are the most pitiful victims of wife abuse. Although the violence is not directed at them personally, they are seriously affected by it nonetheless. Home is the primary classroom for learning how husbands and wives relate to each other and how family disputes are resolved. It is a well-documented fact that children who witness violence between their parents are far more likely to be violent with their own spouses when they reach adulthood.[11] Children watch their parents handling the frustrations and stresses of married life. The responses to conflict they see their parents using become deeply ingrained in their minds. Later, as they imitate parental behavior, they become the next generation of abusive husbands and abused wives.

Because adults in abusive relationships lack adequate communication skills, their children never see dialogue used as a means of overcoming conflict. They never learn the value of open and honest conversation to settle differences of opinion. Instead, they observe that aggression ends disagreements, wins arguments, and goes unpunished. They come to see violence as a legitimate problem-solving tool.

> Studies of the effects of violence and of viewing other people's violence reveal that the more violence you observe, the more tolerant you become of violent behavior. That is not to say that you must use violent behavior yourself. What it does suggest is that you permit it to be used in front of you.[12]

What Is the Father's Role?

Abusive husbands may or may not batter their children. There is some correlation between wife and child abuse; however, not all wife beaters abuse their children. If the children are injured by their father, the wounds may be intentional or unintentional; that is, the children may be beaten in anger or hurt accidentally when they try to intervene in a parental fight. Regardless of whether or not they are physically abused, their father's distorted relationship with their mother causes them grievous emotional harm.

What Is the Abused Mother's Role?

Battered wives tend to feel guilty for failing to provide an ideal home atmosphere for their children. They usually try desperately hard to be good mothers and to make up for the horrors their children witness at home. They shower them with love, protect them, and work at making their lives as secure and safe as possible. They well understand the terror that their small ones experience during their father's rampages. Abused mothers bristle at the thought that even inadvertently their children might be harmed in a domestic dispute. They make arrangements for the children to stay elsewhere when tension is high or warn them to lock themselves in their rooms. They go without certain material comforts in order to provide for their youngsters' needs. They put up with degradation and injury because they feel the children should have a father.

Sometimes the abused woman is so depressed and so needy herself that she reaches a point where she has little or nothing to give her children in the way of love and nurturing. How can she care for them, she wonders, when she can hardly care for herself? She may instead find herself depending on them for strength, in effect, requiring them to be grown up to protect her. In her worst moments, she may take out her frustrations on them, resenting them as a barrier to possible escape.

"Running away myself is one thing. But how can I take three children with me? Who has room to keep us? How could I look for a job?"

Under stress, overwhelmed by her children's ever present needs and demands, she may even abuse them as she herself is abused. On the other hand, the children's welfare may be the very catalyst stimulating her to dare to make a break for it.

"I made the decision to leave after I saw how my kids were being affected. Cookie would take all kinds of abuse from her big brother and then tell me she deserved it! Those kids were acting just like Frank and me. I couldn't let that happen."

WHAT IS THE ABUSIVE HOME'S ENVIRONMENT?

Confusion and Chaos

Children in abusive families have more advantages than their mother. They have contact with the outside world at school and can take comfort in the knowledge that one day they will grow up and be able to leave their violent home. Nevertheless the lives of children in an abusive family are filled with chaos, fear, and suffering. Their most basic emotional needs often go unmet.

A child desperately needs to feel loved, accepted, and safe in order to develop confidence in himself. This confidence builds gradually through the growth of trust between the child and his parents. But an out-of-control father who has the power to frighten and injure the child's mother does not inspire such trust. The child's sense of security is severely strained by witnessing physical brutality toward the woman who is his main source of protection. Denied an environment of physical and emotional safety, a child feels he has no one on whom he can depend. He perceives that his parents are not available to meet his needs. Growing up is very difficult under such circumstances, and many of these children suffer severely for the rest of their lives.

Relationships between members of an abusive family

are distorted and reversed. Children feel they must mother their mother, protect her and themselves from their own father, and withdraw their dependency from both. Their family experiences are entirely different from those of their classmates and friends who do not come from abusive families.

Never-ending Punishments

Frequently and emphatically the literature on abuse states that corporal punishment of children has an adverse effect on them in adulthood. Such punishment, it is said, teaches children that violence toward loved ones is acceptable as long as it is administered for that one's own good. If a loving parent tells his child as he hits him, "I am only doing this because I love you," what else is the child to learn except that loving and hitting can go together and that hitting loved ones may be a good thing under certain circumstances? Because of this, most shelters for battered women have a standing rule that residents must not spank their children.

Some parents take exception to this line of reasoning. Christian parents in particular might quote Scripture to the contrary. "What son is there whom a father does not chasten?" (Heb. 12:7). "He who spares his rod hates his son, but he who loves him disciplines him promptly" (Prov. 13:24).

Sociologist Richard Gelles's research on violence produced an interesting result, which might have some bearing on this issue. He set out to discover which children more often would grow up to be violent spouses, those who were frequently or those who were never hit. His test turned up a startling fact. Children who were never hit became violent adults less often, as he had assumed, but children who were *infrequently* hit (that is less than six times per year) were the least likely of all to grow up to be batterers. Of his test group, approximately

fifty percent of the children who were frequently hit later physically fought with their mates;

90

forty percent of the children who were never hit later physically fought with their mates;

but less than 20 percent of the children who were *infrequently* hit later physically fought with their mates.[13]

One might suggest that a small amount of judiciously applied spanking during childhood produces the most mature adults of all. These adults may be the best equipped to be good mates. They can tolerate frustration—having learned that they cannot always have what they want and do as they please—and they have known the security of loving parents who cared enough to set limits without crushing their children's spirits.

Repeated Behavior Disturbances

What are they like, these children from abusive homes? Can they be readily spotted in school? at play? There is no question that children are affected by their father's abuse of their mother. Living with violence produces inner turmoil that manifests itself in different ways, depending on the age and personality of the child. Each one will cope with life in his own way. However, some basic characteristics appear in children from violent homes.

Infants manifest their awareness of the tension by failing to thrive, eating and sleeping poorly, and crying excessively.

Toddlers and preschoolers generally are terrified when they first witness the beatings, clinging to their mother and trying to push their father away. But they soon learn to fade into the background, to be inconspicuous during a fight. They may actually appear to be unaware of what is happening. Even at this early age they may experience anger toward their helpless mother and decide it is safest to be on their father's side.

The following incident, observed in the playroom of a battered women's shelter, indicates how distorted parent-child relationships can be in abusive homes and how even tiny children struggle for self-preservation by siding with the winner to avoid being destroyed. The child observed here is the three-year-old son of one of the residents.

Tim entered the playroom and sat down at the doll house. He took the father and baby dolls out of the house, leaving the mother and girl dolls behind.

"You're going to jail!" he sternly told the two male dolls and stuck them into a pot of Play-Doh.

"Help, help!" he then called in a higher voice. "The house is burning! Help, help!" The father and baby dolls watched the house burn for a while, then rode away on toy horses, leaving the mother and girl dolls inside.

Tim tipped the house over and dumped everything out onto the floor. He grabbed the girl doll roughly and spanked her hard over and over. He covered her with Play-Doh, pushing as much of it as he could into her underwear. Then he took the mother doll and ripped off her clothes.

"Now you have to lay in the house naked," he said to her. "Everyone is going to look at you." He brought her out of the house and had other dolls and toys carefully look her over.

"I think I'm going to tear your legs off," he told her. He pulled and tugged without success. "I'll pull your head off, too."

He put all the dolls and furniture back inside the house. He then grabbed an ambulance and another doll and brought them over to the house.

"This is the police," he said. "Get out! The house is on fire."

He pulled the father doll from the house and in a small voice called, "Daddy, Daddy! Help, I'm burning up." He pulled the baby doll and a little teddy bear from the "burning" house, gave them a baby bottle full of milk, and set them aside with the father doll. The baby doll said to the father doll, "We'll be all right. But they are burning up!"

He then tipped over the house onto the policeman doll and the ambulance and said, "The cops and everyone else is burning up." He left the toys in a heap and walked away.

When children from violent homes reach school age, other consequences of their distorted lifestyle become apparent. They have learned to be compliant and cooperative with authority figures but may be disruptive and bullying toward other children. Frequent illnesses, hyperactivity, and wanton destructiveness may make them difficult students to cope with. They have difficulty concentrating on school work, but this is understandable considering what awaits them at home. They don't usually talk about their situation. A kind of conspiracy of silence keeps them from confiding in teachers or friends. They believe their way of life is shameful and that no one would believe them anyway.

In an effort to make sense of the violence, they manufacture reasons for their father's brutality. They wonder if their mother did something wrong and deserves her punishment. They wonder if they themselves are somehow to blame.

Adolescents usually take sides with one parent or the other. Some deal with their feelings of fear and powerlessness by placing themselves on their father's side. They may think that because he wins all the fights he is not only powerful but also right. Once they make this choice they must devalue their mother, looking on her with scorn and treating her with the same disrespect their father does.

"Yeah, I hit her sometimes. But she asks for it. She's just plain stupid."

Teen-age girls sometimes choose to side with their mother and see themselves as also worthless and deserving of abuse. They may grow up reluctant to marry and distrustful of all men.

"I'll never make the mistake my mother did. I'm not getting married—ever!"

They may entertain fantasies about rescuing their mother some day.

"As soon as I get old enough, I'm going to do something to him, something he'll never forget."

Still others withdraw from the family altogether, looking forward to the time they can leave it all behind and start fresh on their own.

"Look, it's not my problem. I'm getting out of here just as soon as I can."

Adolescents in particular face certain questions they must answer before they can decide what action to take. Do they have the right to intervene? To whom should they be loyal, mother or father? Do they have the courage to risk injury to themselves in order to protect their mother? What results can they hope for?

In any case, they are forced to cope with the anger they feel toward both parents, with their father for being so cruel and with their mother for being so weak. Sometimes their ability to cope is sorely tested.

If their mother does have their father arrested or if she does separate from him, they may have trouble handling this turn of events. After all, their lives are likely to be seriously disrupted no matter what changes occur. They may end up sharing a crowded shelter, attending a strange school, being separated from their friends, living on a very tight budget, or facing the responsibility for their siblings while their mother works.

Children in the same family will not react in the same way. One may be passive and withdrawn, while another emphatically sides with father or mother. One may be confused and frightened, while another is making careful plans to avenge his mother when he grows up. One may join in the beating, while another stands and calmly watches. Their choice of action is based upon their capacity to understand what is happening and their will to survive.

WHAT IS THE FUTURE FOR CHILDREN FROM ABUSIVE HOMES?

The picture may look grim, but children are resilient. With a little help they may turn out surprisingly well in the end. What they need most is love and security. If the battered mother can recognize how crucial this is and, despite her own needs, see that the children have her love and protection, there is a good chance that they can grow into healthy, mature individuals. (For more about what she can do for them, see chapter 7.)

4

When Did Wife Abuse Begin?

As Christians, we may abhor the problem of domestic violence and know in our hearts that it is wrong for a man to abuse his wife, but we may still be unsure what recourse is legitimately open to the victim, based on God's Word. After all, we evangelicals are committed to the Scripture as God's infallibly inspired revelation of Himself. We know that our allegiance to the Bible is of primary importance in our lives.

Bound by our loyalty to that authority, all our conduct must first pass the test of conforming to scriptural mandates, and we would readily admit that many of these mandates are not easy to understand or to follow. Certain direction in Scripture contradicts our human instincts and our common sense, such as:

> You have heard that it was said, "You shall love your neighbor and hate your enemy." But I say to you, love your enemies, bless those who curse you, do good to those who hate you, and pray for those who spitefully use you and persecute you (Matt. 5:43–44).

But "God works in mysterious ways His wonders to perform." Our basic faith in God's goodness sustains us when we cannot comprehend His purposes.

This faith, however, can be a problem in some circumstances. Couple a basic belief in the inscrutability of God with a superficial and inadequate knowledge of Scripture, and it becomes possible, perhaps even comfortable, to allow certain types of suffering to continue without our interference and with our reluctant blessing.

Take this advice given to the battered woman I

mentioned previously. "God made your husband your lord and master," the two women said. "Even if he tells you to jump out the window, you should do it. If God wants you and your baby to live, don't worry. He'll protect you somehow."

First, they misunderstood the biblical teachings on marriage. Then, in their zeal to defend their point of view, they overlooked another major doctrine.

In His earthly ministry, Christ brought mercy and relief to the suffering wherever He went: "For I have given you an example, that you should do as I have done to you" (John 13:15). Now we are Christ's body in the world, and as such we bear the responsibility for carrying on His work. "He who believes in Me, the works that I do he will do also; and greater works than these he will do" (John 14:12).

Christ may supernaturally intervene in any situation, of course, but that does not negate our duty as His peacemakers, to bring hope and peace and relief from suffering to those who ask.

We dare not say, "God will work it all out," without offering ourselves for His service, for our participation in the lives of the oppressed may be part of His divine plan.

Battered women need our help, but before we can give it we must have an accurate understanding of the situation they face from God's perspective. This chapter and the next will present a picture of marriage, submission, and headship that, while remaining faithful to Scripture, calls for respect and fair treatment for wives and denounces the cruelty and tyranny of abusive husbands.

Male dominance is a major factor in cases of wife abuse. Where husbands see themselves as divinely appointed masters or rulers in the violent household, and where Christian friends, relatives, and helpers of battered women share this view, abused Christian wives stand to be further victimized in the name of the faith. It is crucial that we forever banish the notion that a husband has a God-given right to tyrannize his wife, to force certain behavior from her, or to harm her in any way. No position of leadership or headship justifies abuse. The church must engender in its members an appreciation of marriage that makes marital domination and coercion intolerable.

WHAT WAS GOD'S ORIGINAL PLAN FOR WOMEN?

A single, brief account in the Bible gives a glimpse into God's original plan for marriage, one short moment in the history of humankind when humans were not under the influence of Satan. Although this union was soon marred by sin, a close look at it is helpful in clearing up a common misconception about wives and their "place."

The first chapter of Genesis tells of the creation of the earth. Every part of it was made and pronounced good by its Creator (vv. 4, 10, 12, 18, 21, 25, and 31). Genesis 2 gives further details, specifically concerning the creation of humankind. A man was formed from dust, brought to life by the breath of God, and placed in a beautiful garden as its keeper.

At this point, for the first time, we find God expressing dissatisfaction with something He made (Gen. 2:18). God saw that one thing was not good—the man alone. None of the things Adam was provided with—a flawless environment, creative and fulfilling responsibilities, power, even his personal relationship with almighty God—was sufficient without the human companion God had in mind for him. Beyond all he had, he needed her.

She is described in a short, pithy phrase in verse 18, "an help meet for him" (KJV). From this phrase we have coined the English word *helpmeet* and its daughter, *helpmate*, both used frequently now in referring to spouses in general and wives in particular. The Oxford English Dictionary points out that the word *helpmeet* is "a compound absurdly formed by taking the two words *help meet* in Genesis 2:18–20 as one word." The word *meet*, which follows *help* in the King James Version, means "suitable for, corresponding to, the same as, comparable to." God was making a helper suitable for man.

To us, *helpmeet*, even *helper*, has connotations that

101

cannot be presumed to be present in the Genesis account. Whatever help Adam may have needed, it was not the assistance so many associate with a wife's duties. He surely didn't need a cook, a laundress, or a housekeeper.

Helper and its verb forms occur over 120 times throughout the Old Testament, in all but two cases—those in question here—to describe people and activities that have nothing to do with marriage.

The Hebrew word is *ezer*. It comes from the verb, *azar*, meaning "to surround," hence "to protect or to defend."[1] In order to find out more specifically how the word was used, we can examine the Old Testament application of it.

Who Were the Old Testament Helpers?

Isaiah 30:5 records that the Israelites, fearing attack from their enemies the Assyrians, formed an alliance with an Egyptian pharaoh, asking him to be their helper.

In Joshua 1:14, Joshua, preparing to cross the Jordan and take his people into the Promised Land, instructed the fighting men from the tribes of Gad, Manasseh, and Reuben to leave their possessions and families behind and cross over with the other tribes to be helpers in the battles to conquer this territory.

First Chronicles 18:5 tells of an alliance Hadadezer, king of Zobah, made with the army of the Arameans to help them win their war against King David. The Arameans became the helpers of Hadadezer.

In the biblical list of helpers, impressive in its tally of the strong, the mighty, and the valiant, the most significant has been left until last.

> Behold, God is my helper;
> The LORD is with those who uphold my life
>   (Ps. 54:4).

> I will lift my eyes to the hills—
> From whence comes my help?
> My help comes from the LORD,
> Who made heaven and earth (Ps. 121:1–2).

Our soul waits for the LORD;
He is our help and our shield (Ps. 33:20).

But I am poor and needy;
Make haste to me, O God!
You are my help and my deliverer;
O LORD, do not delay (Ps 70:5).

More than sixty times God is called man's helper.
The help He gives is protection, strengthening, preservation of life, defense against capture, prevention of destruction, and His comforting presence in times of disaster.

Where "help" is used in reference to humans helping each other, the ideas are similar, suggesting a partnership or a protective alliance against enemies. Only in Genesis 2 do we find the word used of a woman, and there it refers to Eve, designated by God to be man's helper. She was not created an insignificant assistant; she was an ally. Without her, Adam's existence was not perfect. As God's provision for man, she was indispensable to his well-being. Her role is not to be belittled or scorned, for she shared her office with God, who is also man's helper.

Did Adam understand all this? Indeed he did. Genesis 2:23 records his words when he first saw her, but the English rendition of the verse inadequately conveys his depth of feeling. His excitement is partially lost when the original Hebrew text is translated in complete sentences. Actually, the grammar of the verse is jumbled and chaotic, indicating a certain speechless surprise and joy.[2] He is incoherent with delight as he recognizes in the woman what he has not seen in any animal—kinship to himself. He notes that her body and his are the same. Then he pronounces his name and hers, *ish* and *isshah*, "man" and "woman." His words demonstrate his understanding that she is not an inferior by-product of himself, but another likeness of him, a perfect match.[3]

This was marriage in the beginning. Within the evangelical community we must guard against giving husbands a position of unlimited supremacy based on this passage. The right of the male to dominate by means of coercion or tyranny cannot be substantiated from this passage.

WHAT HAPPENED TO GOD'S PLAN AFTER THE FALL?

The idyllic conditions described in Genesis 2 were short-lived, for in Genesis 3 we read about man's fall into sin. Although disobedience did not destroy marriage completely, sin brought some devastating changes in man that seriously affected the marriage relationship.

All kinds of evil flooded God's serene creation, wreaking havoc in nature, in Adam and Eve's marriage, and in the realm of man's relationship to God. The destructive power of sin was evident everywhere.

The first negative effect recorded is the loss of intimacy between the man and the woman (Gen. 3:7). Before their disobedience Adam and Eve had been completely comfortable and at ease with each other, naked and unashamed (Gen. 2:25). As soon as they ate the forbidden fruit, they became self-conscious and made clothes for themselves from leaves. The wonderful, easy familiarity between them was gone. In clothing themselves they demonstrated that communion was broken and a curtain of separation had dropped between them.

The second negative effect on the marriage was a loss of loyalty (Gen. 3:12). Adam blamed Eve for being the cause of his sin. Their partnership, their alliance, and their oneness were no longer. Adam was now looking out for himself alone.

The consequences of sin fell equally on the man and the woman. They suffered a broken relationship with each other and with God. The beautiful world they had been born into was now subject to decay, and their previously infinite creative potential was diminished. God enumerated for them some of the changes that would occur as a result of the introduction of sin into their lives.

To the woman He said:

"I will greatly multiply your sorrow and your
conception;
In pain you shall bring forth children;
Your desire shall be for your husband,
And he shall rule over you."
Then to Adam He said. . . .
"Cursed is the ground for your sake;
In toil you shall eat of it all the days of your life.
Both thorns and thistles it shall bring forth for you,
And you shall eat the herb of the field.
In the sweat of your face, you shall eat bread
Till you return to the ground,
For out of it you were taken;
For dust you are, and to dust you shall return"
(Gen. 3:16–19).

Their once flawless world was now full of hardships.
With sin came pain—for the woman, pain in childbearing.

The noted British obstetrician, Grantly Dick-Read,
who wrote extensively on the subject of childbirth, maintained there is no anatomical reason for the pain that
invariably accompanies the birth of a baby. "The physio-
logical perfection of the human body knows no greater
paradox than pain in parturition," he wrote.[4] He pointed
out that the mechanism of delivery is a simple process of
muscle contraction and muscle relaxation, processes we
use for all motion and body function, normally without
discomfort. Yet, modern medical techniques notwithstand-
ing, labor and delivery of an infant are painful. It seems
reasonable to assume that the pain is one of the distortions
of God's original creation. The Lord did not intend for
birthing to be hurtful; the pain came with sin.

The writer of Genesis makes the further point that
despite the agony of childbearing, women will long for
marriage. They will desire the intimacy of the love
relationship although the eventual outcome is painful. That
will not be the only pain they bear, for their husbands will
tend to domineer over them. The once perfect alliance and
partnership will give way to an inclination to overpower
and control. This is perhaps the crowning blow—the

mistreatment that will fall on women at the hands of the very men whom they love, oppression from the ones meant to be intimate companions, allies, and friends.

The accuracy of this prediction can be deduced from even the most cursory examination of the history of women. No single verse of Scripture more clearly describes the relationship between an abusive husband and his wife than does Genesis 3:16. Although the woman loves and desires her husband, the effects of sin are such that he takes advantage of this love and "lords it over her" (Jerusalem Bible). Even when, beaten and in despair, she finds her love turning to distrust, her dependence on him continues. Terror may lead her to accept his bullying in an effort to appease him. God's omniscient prediction at the dawn of time has been realized billions of times over since then and is commonplace even in our day.

Three points need to be made when relating this passage to wife abuse. First, the words of Genesis 3:16 do not constitute God's will for the treatment of wives by their husbands. God's words in this passage are predictive, not prescriptive. There is only one prescription for sin, and that remedy was foretold in Genesis 3:15, where God told the serpent Satan that the offspring of a woman would do away with him. Christ is that offspring.

God's statements to the man and the woman were predictive explanations, to them and to us, of how sin would disturb His original creation. Theologian H. C. Leupold says: "God is not here issuing a special commandment, 'Be thou ruled over by him!' or 'Thou shalt not rule!' But here in Genesis 3:16 we have a statement, a prediction, a prophecy, of how man, degenerated by sin, would take advantage of his headship as a husband to dominate, lord it over, his wife."[5]

Many Christians have misinterpreted these words of Genesis 3 to the detriment of women. Verse 16 has even been called "the first commandment which God gave unto woman."[6] Such an idea couldn't be further from the truth. This is not a commandment. There is nothing a woman could do on the basis of this phrase. Had God had this intention, He would have needed to inform her husband, "Rule over your wife!" He would have told the woman, "Obey your husband!" But the statement is not couched in the imperative. God is simply speaking of the future and saying that this, sadly, is what is going to happen.[7]

Second, notice the use of the word *rule*. This word in Hebrew is used of kings over their subjects and means "to have power over, to order about, to reign." An example of this usage occurs in Judges 8:23: "But Gideon said to them, 'I will not rule over you, nor shall my son rule over you; the LORD shall rule over you.'" When used of a wicked ruler, it implies tyranny: "When the righteous are in authority, the people rejoice; But when a wicked man rules, the people groan" (Prov. 29:2).

Nowhere in Scripture can we find a command to husbands to rule over their wives in this manner. In fact, Jesus repeatedly warns His followers against this type of behavior:

> You know that those who are considered rulers over the Gentiles lord it over them, and their great ones exercise authority over them. Yet it shall not be so among you; but whoever desires to become great among you shall be your servant. And whoever of you desires to be first shall be slave of all (Mark 10:42–44).

Christ's call to leadership is a call to servanthood; He Himself is the prime example. The concept of ruling does not constitute God's intent for husbands and has no place in Christian marriage.

The third point pertinent to abusive marriages concerns the Christian response to sin. Because a husband's lording it over his wife is a result of sin, Christians should work as hard to eradicate it from the world as they work to eradicate the other negative effects of the Fall.

The presence of evil did not affect only Eve. Adam, too, suffered from sin's entry into the garden. The ground grew thorns and thistles. Cultivating and managing the earth turned to drudgery. It became Adam's lot to work himself to sweaty exhaustion to provide for his family. In the end, he was told, he would die and his body return to dust.

One point of view suggests that while the domination of woman by man described in Genesis 3:16 is *not* God's best, it represents His second best. When sin came into the world, proponents of this theory say, God's peaceable creation erupted into chaos and He was forced to institute a hierarchy for the good of humankind and the sake of order. Man's domination of woman became necessary because it helped restore harmony in the world. Since it is God's plan, we dare not tamper with it.

If we use this reasoning in reference to man's domination over woman, we must also apply it to the other aspects of God's pronouncements recorded in Genesis 3. Thorns and thistles become God's second best, too, and the use of herbicides must be condemned as an attempt to tamper with His will. Exhausting and arduous labor become God's will, and man dare not shirk his God-given responsibility to sweat and toil in his work. Thus, all conveniences and labor-saving devices thwart God's purposes.

These ideas seem preposterous. Farmers wouldn't farm without weed-killers to increase their productivity and to improve the quality of their crops. Nobody wants to give up the luxuries that reduce "the sweat of his brow." Are those who refuse medical treatment obeying God's will better than those who care for their bodies when they are ill?

Yet, for many years the results of the Fall that particularly affected women were seen in another light. At one time analgesia and anesthesia were withheld from laboring women because of God's "curse" of pain in childbearing.[8] Even though that has changed in recent years, today well-intentioned people still use the last phrase of Genesis 3:16, "and he shall rule over you," not as a sad picture of the effects of sin on the marriage relationship, not as something to be overcome or to be fought against, but as a picture of God's will.

In dealing with marriage problems among Christians,

we should clearly understand that there is no basis for claiming that domination by man over woman is God-sanctioned in this Genesis passage. Genesis 3:16 does not demonstrate God's desire that woman be dominated by her partner.

If you are a battered woman and have been wrestling in your own mind about your responsibility as a Christian wife, rest assured. Nothing in the second or third chapters of Genesis in any way condemns you to a life of abuse at the hands of your mate.

What Are Some Other Theories?

Some anthropologists, claiming that the human race came into existence under adverse conditions of climate and geography, maintain that humans survived from the beginning through violence. The survival of the strong came at the expense of the weak. Males, physically stronger, abducted females to be their mates, dragging them off to their lairs caveman-style. They kept control over women by force.[9]

Susan Brownmiller, author of *Against Our Will: Men, Women, and Rape*, sees things differently. She asserts that early humans were a completely promiscuous lot, cohabiting at will and leading a generally frantic and barbarous life. Women were held in high regard as the only known parents of the children. At some point in the chaos, Brownmiller believes, women, physically unable to protect themselves from the stronger men, voluntarily gave up their freedom for a monogamous relationship, hoping this pairing would protect them from rape. With the advent of one-man / one-woman couples, men took over power in the family, becoming brutal masters and treating their wives as property.[10]

Another explanation of the origin of wife abuse speaks of early man as a worshiper of the female in deity form. Early man revered things female and built myths around a great goddess who coupled with a snake to produce the world. Many years later, it is said, the misogynist Hebrews stole the snake idea and rewrote the myths, making the male the superior sex.[11] In this explanation, the Bible carries the responsibility for institutionalizing the inferiority of women. Some texts in Genesis, Ephesians, and 1 Peter are quoted out of context to prove the point.

What Do Christians Believe?

But Christians can see Genesis as the true account of the devastating effects of evil on the world, and thus wife abuse becomes a distortion of the marriage relationship. As such it deserves to be obliterated along with Satan's other lies.

5

"Wives, Submit Yourselves to. . . ."

For the Christian who is looking for an answer to the problem of wife abuse, probably no scriptural issue is more important than submission. Evangelicals concerned about domestic violence are frequently disconcerted by what they see as the Bible's demand that an abused woman put up with assault and degradation. The often-preached words, "Wives, submit to your own husbands, as to the Lord" (Eph. 5:22), ring in their ears and hang over their heads as they attempt to find a compassionate as well as orthodox solution to the problem of battering.

The idea exists that battering is the just and legitimate consequence of failing to submit to one's husband. After hearing the pitiful story of an abused woman for the first time, many people—counselors and pastors, relatives, and friends—struggling to make sense from such tragedy, search for a logical cause for her mistreatment. There has to be a reason. "She must not be submitting," they decide. They consider the well-known Scripture references to proper wifely conduct and conclude that the root of the trouble in her marriage is her rebellious and insubordinate spirit. It seems to fit and it makes sense. After all, God ordained that a wife should submit to her husband. When she does, He rewards her by causing her husband to treat her well. This has become a standard theory for Christian wives. Husbands need to feel they are the boss. God has given them this position. If wives are not submissive, *it is only natural* for their husbands to become angry and abusive. When a stubborn, nagging, bossy wife gives up such behavior and treats her husband the way he is supposed to be treated, the abuse will stop and the marriage will take on all the characteristics of the beautiful heavenly union it was meant to be.

The reality, however, is quite different. Unsubmissive behavior does not *cause* a husband to beat his wife, and submissive behavior does not *cause* him to stop. Abused women are submissive women. Their whole lives are wrapped up in pleasing their mates. That, in one sense, is the tragedy. If these women really were rebellious, emasculating shrews, they could fight back or leave their abusive husbands without a qualm, and that would at least be one solution to the problem.

Instead, battered women keep trying to satisfy their unreasonable spouses. "What am I doing wrong, Honey? Just tell me what I should do," they plead. And the abuse continues.

The more a woman endures, the more she tells her husband that what he is doing is acceptable, that she deserves it, and that he is right to "punish" her or "teach her a lesson." Rather than providing a solution, further submission perpetuates a lie and reinforces the husband's motivation to humiliate and injure his wife.

The idea of submission of one mate to the other is certainly not wrong. Submission is a biblical concept, of that there can be no doubt. God hates arrogance and loves humility. But the emphasis that demands only *wifely* submission is wrong, and it has been used for years to place a special burden on women that men do not share.

When we examine the Scripture, we find that *all* believers are required to display this attitude and conduct toward one another. "Be filled with the Spirit . . . submitting to one another in the fear of God" (Eph. 5:18, 21). "Yes, all of you be submissive to one another, and be clothed with humility, for 'God resists the proud, but gives grace to the humble' " (1 Peter 5:5).

Christians are expected to yield their own rights for the good of others, to look out for the interests of the other members of the body of Christ, and to show respect for fellow Christians. These are general responsibilities of the Christian life that all believers share.

Beyond the general call to all believers to submit to one another, the descriptions of the particular duties of husbands to their wives also suggest that the responsibilities of headship should be carried out in a spirit of submission. Paul tells husbands to love their wives in a self-sacrificial way, looking after them as tenderly as they would their own bodies, nourishing and cherishing them (Eph. 5:25–29). They are to spare nothing—not even their own lives—in caring for their mates. Peter tells husbands to "honor" their wives and treat them with understanding (1 Peter 3:7). Neither apostle tells husbands to dominate or control their wives but rather to follow Christ's example of self-giving love. Christ gave Himself to redeem the church, to cause her to grow to become beautiful and strong, and to lead her into everlasting life.

Misuse of Scripture unwittingly encourages some husbands "to be selfish, egocentric, convinced of [their] right to have [their] own way and filled with pride and a heady sense of power. . . . No person can remain unspoiled by the corrupting effect of power when he is told he holds by divine right a position of superiority in which others are duty bound to subject themselves to him."[1]

Al came to a pastoral counseling center as a last resort when his wife threatened to leave him. The couple talked over their problems with a counselor, and before long it came out that Al abused Terri, that even though other conflicts had been discussed first, this was her reason for leaving.

"Look," Al said defensively, "I'm a Christian husband, and I try to live up to the standards of conduct set out in the Bible. I'm head of my home, and I bear the responsibility for what goes on there. I have a right to have my way—the Bible gives me that right. Terri has to submit to me and obey me. When she doesn't do what I say, it is up to me to see that she does. She has to do things my way. I'm responsible."

For couples like Al and Terri, mutual submission has turned into one-sided exploitation. When this happens, something must be done to break the unhealthy patterns for the sake of both mates and their children, because nothing could be further from the biblical standard Christ established.

CHRIST SUBMITTED HIMSELF TO. . . .

Jesus was the perfect model of submission. "Let this mind be in you which was also in Christ Jesus, [who] . . . humbled Himself and became obedient to the point of death, even the death of the cross" (Phil. 2:5, 8).

He chose to submit to residing in an infant's body, to growing up as a boy under the authority of human parents, to enduring the abuse of a criminal's death at the hands of those He loved. His submission had a special, eternal purpose—our redemption, our salvation. All that He endured was to that end.

Jesus yielded to abuse when it served the purpose for which He came. But He made it clear to those to whom He submitted that He did so voluntarily, from a position of strength.

In the Garden of Gethsemane when He was arrested, He reminded His followers that He had His own means of escape at His disposal if He wished to be rescued. Jesus said, "Do you think that I cannot now pray to My Father, and He will provide Me with more than twelve legions of angels?" (Matt. 26:53).

During His trial Jesus corrected Pilate when he said he had the power to have Jesus killed or released. Jesus stated, "You could have no power at all against Me unless it had been given you from above" (John 19:11).

The submission of an abused woman, however, is neither voluntary nor from a position of strength. Although she begins her married life eager to please her husband in every way, the abuse she suffers soon changes her service from voluntary to terror-induced. What she offered freely and lovingly at first is later taken from her by force.

All the humiliation and pain might still be worthwhile

if it served some purpose, if it led to the conversion of even one lost soul. Does submission to a demanding, brutal husband result in his eventual spiritual awakening, as some hope? Unfortunately, no.

A WIFE SUBMITS HERSELF TO....

A wife's humble surrender to abuse merely increases her husband's contempt for her. Her compliance tells him that she agrees with him, that she is as inadequate and as in need of domination as he says. All his erroneous attitudes of superiority, disgust, and scorn are confirmed by her behavior. He despises her weakness.

> "If a husband is allowed to continue [abusive] behavior without experiencing any negative consequences, why should he change?" asks Christian counselor Norman Wright. "He is simply being allowed to get away with something and in many cases his respect for his wife is lessened."[2]

Pastor/author Louis Evans, Jr., concurs.

> After listening to some of the things such husbands demand of their wives ... I am convinced that a wife only reinforces her husband's arrogance and demeans herself by submitting to him. Nobody wins by such appeasement.[3]

Submission is not a state of mindless subservience in all situations. Jesus Himself did not always submit in every crisis He faced. He did not submit when to do so would force Him to concede to evil. He did not submit to the desecration of His Father's house (see Mark 11). Merchants legally sold their goods there with the blessing of the religious authorities—the same authorities to whom He would submit at a later time. These dishonest and greedy men were defiling a holy place, and Christ attacked them and threw them out.

It is the same with the abused woman. Her call to submit to her husband does not compel her to comply with evil. "Do you not know that you are the temple of God and that the Spirit of God dwells in you? If anyone defiles the temple of God, God will destroy him. For the temple of God is holy, which temple you are" (1 Cor. 3:16–17).

As Norman Wright goes on to say,

> Some have taught that a wife should submit to beatings, but I cannot see that violating one teaching of Scripture to fulfill another makes sense. If our bodies are the temple of the Holy Spirit then we ought not to do anything that would bring harm to the body. That includes allowing one spouse to beat the other.[4]

A Christian woman's first allegiance is to Christ. She submits to His authority over her and His wishes for her first. No one stands between her and her Lord. All other duties and loyalties come second.

Jesus never submitted without good and sufficient reason. Luke 4 recounts an incident from the beginning of Jesus' ministry when He went to Nazareth and stood in the synagogue to read. He proclaimed Himself the Lord's Anointed One, Messiah, and the people in the place became enraged. Dragging Him outside, they headed for a cliff and tried to throw Him off the edge. But it was not yet His time to die for them, and He escaped. Submission in that case would have been for nothing.

In the years following Jesus' death and resurrection, His apostles also taught submission as a pattern of behavior for Christians. Again, submission was always to serve a purpose.

WIVES IN THE BIBLE TIMES SUBMITTED THEMSELVES TO. . . .

Submission was to give the world a picture of the beautiful relationship existing between Christ and His bride, the church. Paul finished his Ephesians discourse on husbands and wives by saying, "This is a great mystery, but I speak concerning Christ and the church" (Eph. 5:32).

As in the Old Testament where Jehovah described himself as the faithful husband of Israel, here Paul pointed to marriage as a way of communicating to the world what the relationship of Christ is to the church. In the world in which Paul lived, where husbands were powerful and sometimes brutal masters answering to no one, imagine the witness that was provided by Christian husbands who put their wives' welfare ahead of their own and cherished and loved them tenderly. Nonbelievers truly envisioned Christ's love for His own from such a demonstration.

Within marriage, the purpose of a Christian wife's submission was to serve as a witness to her nonbelieving husband. Peter declared, "Likewise you wives, be submissive to your own husbands, that even if some do not obey the word, they, without a word, may be won by the conduct of their wives" (1 Peter 3:1). Peter was anxious that Christian women not nag or pester their husbands about their new faith but rather live in such a way that their actions might speak for them.

Submission within the body of Christ is to bring about harmony, spiritual maturity, and the growth of each member. "With all lowliness and gentleness, with long-suffering, bearing with one another in love, endeavoring to keep the unity of the Spirit in the bond of peace. . . . till we all come to the unity of the faith and the knowledge of the Son of God" (Eph. 4:2, 3, 13).

Still another purpose for submission was expounded by Peter and Paul. Peter said, "Therefore submit yourselves to every ordinance of man for the Lord's sake, whether to the king as supreme, or to governors. . . . For this is the will of God, that by doing good you may put to silence the ignorance of foolish men" (1 Peter 2:13–15). Paul told Titus that the younger women in his church should be "subject to their own husbands, that the Word of God may not be dishonored" (Titus 2:5 NASB). Peter and Paul were concerned that the reputations of Christians be spotless and that the integrity of the gospel be maintained.

BATTERED WOMEN SUBMIT THEMSELVES TO. . . .

In relating this understanding of submission to the situation of the battered woman, it may be helpful to determine if endurance of continued emotional, physical, and sexual abuse by one's husband accomplishes any of the specified purposes for which such behavior is recommended in Scripture.

First, the picture of Christ and the church: An abusive marriage certainly doesn't represent that relationship.

Second, the possible conversion of an unbelieving mate: As has already been pointed out, the abusive husband reacts to his wife's submission with more abuse and contempt, not contrition and repentance.

Third, harmony between believers and spiritual growth: The wife who allows her husband to continue to perpetrate criminal acts against her is not contributing to his welfare or growth. It is not in his best interests for her to allow their relationship to deteriorate into a terrorist versus hostage situation. Her submission destroys him as surely as his assaults destroy her.

Fourth, the reputation of the gospel: The abused woman finds public regard for her and her faith waning if she continues to permit herself to be mistreated. The longer the situation goes unchanged, the longer the woman tolerates abuse without making a move to end it, the more her friends and relatives feel their concern for her ebbing. What is the matter with her, they ask themselves, that she allows herself to be so ill-used? Skepticism turns finally to disgust and abandonment. She becomes an object of contempt. Even her children find themselves drawn more and more away from their mother when she does nothing to help herself. They feel betrayed by her because she will not stand up and be strong for them. They want and need security and protection, and she provides neither. Eventually they, too, give up on her and either turn to imitating their father or withdraw from the family altogether.

Nor does the abused Christian woman's submission, a product of her Christian faith, protect the integrity of the gospel message, for in despising her, people despise *it*, too. What kind of religion, they wonder, demands that a person degrade herself in such a way?

In short, the final disastrous effects of unchecked abuse may include condemnation and contempt from her husband, the disillusionment and "burn out" of family and friends, the withdrawal and rejection by her children, and disparagement of her faith by all.

Because submission then perpetuates abuse and accomplishes no good, some other response to abuse must be found for the Christian woman. Peter and Paul simply refused to submit when submission was inappropriate. When the rulers, elders, scribes, and high priests at Jerusalem forbade Peter and John to preach the gospel, they did not yield to that authority. "And they called them and commanded them not to speak at all nor teach in the name of Jesus. But Peter and John answered and said to them, 'Whether it is right in the sight of God to listen to you more than to God, you judge. For we cannot but speak the things which we have seen and heard'" (Acts 4:18–20). Although Peter believed strongly that Christians should be exemplary in their conduct and in their obedience to governing authorities (see 1 Peter 2:13–15), he could not submit to demands that would have a negative effect on the spread of the gospel.

Paul also emphatically stated it was a Christian's duty to submit to governing authority: "Therefore whoever resists the authority resists the ordinance of God" (Rom. 13:2). He wrote in his letter to the Philippians that Christians should imitate Christ who submitted to a criminal's ignominious death.

Yet in Acts 16, Paul himself did not submit to the wishes of the magistrates who had unjustly imprisoned him.

> So the keeper of the prison reported these words to Paul, saying, "The magistrates have sent to let you go. Now therefore depart, and go in peace." But Paul said to them, "They have beaten us openly, uncondemned Romans, and have thrown us into prison. And now do they put us out secretly? No, indeed! Let them come themselves and get us out" (Acts 16:36–37).

Submission is supposed to accomplish something positive. When its effect would be negative, we may choose not to submit. Peter and John had to refuse to submit in order to continue to preach Christ. Paul had to refuse to submit in order to protect his integrity as a minister of the gospel.

What of the battered woman? She is called, as all wives are called, to submit to her husband. This is a clear and repeated message in the Epistles. When she can submit without ignoring her primary allegiance to the Lord, she should. But she must not allow herself to support or encourage a relationship with her husband that desecrates the picture of Christ's relationship to the church. She must not tolerate a situation that renders her incapable of raising her children in the nurture and admonition of the Lord. She must not by her passiveness become an accessory to her husband's acts of assault and battery.

"In such a case as this, a woman ought to calmly let her husband know (when they are not fighting) that if he ever lays another hand upon her, she will either notify the police and sign a complaint against him or separate from him," says Wright.[5]

There are ways in which an abused Christian woman *can* submit, however. Although she flees from her husband and lets him know that she will no longer be a party to illegal acts of violence, she *can* tell him she wants to return to him as soon as he obtains professional help and has his behavior under control. She can conduct herself decently and with dignity during the separation, not defiantly or vengefully, not returning evil for evil, insult for insult. She can demonstrate a quiet and gentle spirit.

Submission is an essential ingredient in the life of every Christian, and it is not put aside or discredited here. But a kind of submission that requires a woman to yield passively to assault and degradation is *not the answer to the problem of domestic violence*.

WHO IS THE WIFE'S HEAD?

In their research on family violence, Straus, Gelles, and Steinmetz found that a large amount of physical violence between mates was related to attempts on the husband's part to maintain a superior power position. In other words, men used violence as a way of demonstrating to themselves and to others that they were indeed in charge.

"You shut your mouth, you hear, or I'll shut it for you. No woman is going to tell me what to do in my own house."

"Every woman needs a good swift kick in the backside now and again because they have a tendency, you know, to get too big for their britches, and you have to keep them in their place."

"You've got to make sure you never let her get too smug, son. You've got to keep reminding her who's boss around here."

Abusive men are men who desperately need to be in charge. Their violence is partly due to a cultural norm equating masculinity, headship, and the use of physical strength. Subtle teaching during childhood urges little boys to be rough and aggressive, to fight for what they want. As a result they learn that the way to be masculine is to be violent.

Who Is the Wife's Head, Traditionally Speaking?

Traditional views of marital sex roles also lend support to the use of force. Men who are given the go-ahead to be the supreme authority at home then expect everything to go their way. They want the last say in every discussion; they want to make all the decisions. Physical violence seems justified to them if they need help in maintaining this level of authority. Eventually abuse comes to be perceived as normal male behavior.

Our heroes exhibit this kind of behavior, and it always seems to work for them. In order to regain control over his wife, for example, the cattle baron (John Wayne) spanks his obstreperous, rebellious wife (Maureen O'Hara), and although she screams and protests, the treatment does her a lot of good. After the disciplining, husband and wife, happily reconciled, walk off arm in arm into the sunset.[6]

Add the approval of Scripture to society's acceptance of violence, and the result is a deadly combination indeed.

"Nearly every abusive husband I counsel, Christian or not, at some time or other tries to justify himself by quoting the Bible," says one men's counselor at a shelter for battered women. "They say, 'The Bible says a man is the head of his wife. So I have the God-given right to do to her as I please.'"

Scripture passages dealing with marriage and headship have been misused for years to justify male selfishness. When the Bible calls the man of the house the leader or the head, it is not referring to what we commonly understand as leadership—aggression and dominance; instead, it is referring to imitation of God's relationship to Israel and Christ's relationship to the church. That is an entirely different thing.

Who Is the Wife's Head, Biblically Speaking?

The distinction between domination and husbandly leadership appears first in the Old Testament. God sent the prophet Hosea to Israel with a message for His unfaithful people. Hosea told them of the future restoration God had planned for them. God was looking ahead to the day when He would tenderly lead Israel back to Himself, and He spoke these words:

> I will allure her . . . And speak comfort to her. . . . I will give her her vineyards. . . . And it shall be, in that day . . . that you will call Me "My Husband" and no longer call Me "My Master" . . . I will betroth you to Me forever . . . in loving-kindness and mercy (Hosea 2:14–19).

God distinguishes here between the actions of a master and those of a husband, as He explains His future relationship to Israel. Among the latter, love and tenderness are foremost, and domination is nowhere to be found. God exhibits patient, faithful, enduring love for His spouse and continues to love her despite her shortcomings. Human earthly marriage ought to represent on earth what this divine relationship is like. "As the bridegroom rejoices over the bride, So shall your God rejoice over you" (Isa. 62:5).

In the New Testament, Christ's relationship with His church is our pattern for leadership in marriage. Paul calls husbands to be the heads of their wives as Christ is the head of the church. That headship is based on a relationship to total giving of Himself—His very life. It is described in such terms in Ephesians 5: Christ gave Himself for us "an offering and a sacrifice to God" (v. 2); "He is the Savior of the body" (v. 23); "Christ also loved the church and gave Himself for it" (v. 25).

This headship involves nurturing and building up one's wife, giving to her as opposed to demanding from her. "So husbands ought to love their own wives as their own bodies; he who loves his wife loves himself. For no one ever hated his own flesh, but nourishes and cherishes it, just as the Lord does the church" (Eph. 5:28–29).

Leadership among Christians is always the opposite of leadership in the world. The Christian leader is a servant, not a master. "And do not be called teachers; for One is your teacher, the Christ. But he who is greatest among you shall be your servant" (Matt. 23:10–11).

Christian leadership is not a matter of exercising power over another but of using authority with a servant attitude. Christ Himself demonstrated the requirements of leadership while He was on earth. He said, "You call me Teacher and Lord, and you say well, for so I am. If I then, your Lord and Teacher, have washed your feet, you also ought to wash one another's feet. For I have given you an example, that you should do as I have done to you" (John 13:13–15).

The matter of headship is illustrated by the manner in which Christ leads the church. He never bullies or overpowers, never forces or coerces. He leads only insofar as the church is willing to be led. He never breaks down the door but stands patiently knocking (see Rev. 3:20).

Biblical headship, then, is Christlike servanthood and sacrifice. It is leadership by example, quite a contrast to aggressive rulership. When the term *rule* is used in connection with families in the New Testament, it adds a very positive dimension to the idea of husbandly headship.

In 1 Timothy 3, Paul gives instructions for choosing church leaders. Each must be above reproach. Each must be "one who rules his own house well" (v. 4). It is important to our understanding of headship that we correctly interpret this word *rule*.

The Greek word is *proistemi*, which means "to stand before as a protector, a guardian, a patron, a champion." Headship involves all these things. Husbands are to protect their families, to guard them against the evil influences of the world. As a patron advocates for and advances a cause, so the husband is to promote the welfare of his wife and family, always taking care to act in their best interests. As their champion, he fights for them, defending and supporting them against all who might threaten them. He energetically seeks their safety and security, their physical and spiritual well-being.

In some ways the commonly held evangelical view of marital roles constitutes a part of the problem of wife abuse rather than contributing to its resolution. This view must change. Mindless, fear-induced, one-sided wifely submission and coercive, authoritarian male leadership do not represent the biblical model of marriage. Until believers commit themselves to conduct that is truly Christian, abuse will continue in the church.

6

Should the Suffering Wife Seek Deliverance?

If I cry out concerning wrong,
I am not heard.
If I cry aloud there is no justice.

He has fenced up my way,
So that I cannot pass. . . .

He breaks me down on every side,
And I am gone. . . .

My relatives have failed,
And my close friends have forgotten me. . . .

Even young children despise me;
I arise, and they speak against me. . . .

Have pity on me, have pity on me,
O you my friends (Job 19:7, 8, 10, 14, 18, 21).

WHAT IS SUFFERING FOR AN ABUSED WIFE?

Suffering is a universal experience, borne by the godly and the wicked alike. Insecurity, anguish, fear, pain, sorrow, and death all entered the world with sin and have been plaguing man ever since. When the question is asked, "Why do people suffer?" a complete answer is impossible, but Scripture seems to offer some explanations.

First, there is, of course, the direct connection between sin and suffering. God said to Cain, "The voice of your brother's blood cries out to Me. . . . So now you are cursed. . . . When you till the ground, it shall no longer yield its strength to you. A fugitive and a vagabond you shall be on the earth" (Gen. 4:10–12).

Second, suffering is a by-product of the activity of Satan. "Then Satan went out from the presence of the Lord, and struck Job with painful boils from the sole of his foot to the crown of his head" (Job 2:7).

Third, suffering is sometimes part of a plan to reveal the glory of God. John 9:1–7 tells the story of a blind man made to see. The disciples asked Jesus whether it was the sin of the man himself or the sin of his parents that caused him to be born blind. Jesus stretched their thinking with His reply: "Neither this man nor his parents sinned, but that the works of God should be revealed in him"(v. 3).

Fourth, suffering is also presented in the Scripture as a tool to mature and refine God's children, to equip us to do His work.

> We also glory in tribulations, knowing that tribulation produces perseverance; and perseverance, character; and character, hope (Rom. 5:3–4).

129

Blessed be the God and Father of our Lord Jesus Christ, the Father of mercies and God of all comfort, who comforts us in all our tribulation, that we may be able to comfort those who are in any trouble, with the comfort with which we ourselves are comforted by God (2 Cor. 1:3–4).

How do these reasons for suffering apply to the situation of the abused Christian woman? Is she being punished for some sin? Is Satan at work around her? Will her suffering bring glory to God? Is it meant to mature and refine her?

Regrettably, many evangelical Christians interpret most suffering as a punishment for sin—the fault of the sufferer, the result of personal wrongdoing and retribution from the Lord. However, through Jesus Christ's death and resurrection, God's wrath against believers has been canceled. We are justified through faith in His Son. Our sin is wiped away, and we no longer face God's anger. Two assurances of this fact are found in the book of Romans. "Therefore, having been justified by faith, we have peace with God through our Lord Jesus Christ" (Rom. 5:1). "There is therefore now no condemnation to those who are in Christ Jesus" (Rom. 8:1). The Christian woman whose husband beats her need not fear that the Lord is punishing her. He has redeemed her; she is acquitted of all wrong-doing.

Can her sufferings then be regarded as disciplinary, the actions of a loving Father toward His daughter, as it says in Hebrews 12? "For whom the Lord loves He chastens, and scourges every son whom He receives. If you endure chastening, God deals with you as with sons"(Heb. 12:6–7).

Difficult circumstances may be regarded as disciplinary, to be sure, but we must go slowly in using this interpretation to keep a woman locked within an abusive situation. Some suffering may have as its purpose to bring a defect or failing to our attention or to teach us and help us grow spiritually. It is an important distinction to make, however, that these ideas do not mean we cannot seek to be released from suffering. Remember Paul himself was subject to such an instructive measure, what he called his "thorn in the flesh." He earnestly sought relief from it. It was only when no relief was forthcoming that he was satisfied to endure it "that the power of Christ may rest upon me" (2 Cor. 12:9). We can profit from our suffering, learn from it, grow through it, and still be doing all we can to escape it.

Evil is always at war with good, which may very well be the origin of many a battered woman's anguish. Not until Satan is crushed forever will we see an end to suffering on this earth, but God does not stand by helplessly as Satan ravages humankind with his evil power. God's power supersedes all other power. The battered Christian woman can take comfort in knowing He turns evil to good for those who love Him, and He causes His name to be glorified.

Nor is God insensitive to the suffering we encounter, whatever its purpose. Suffering, even when it is arranged for His glory, causes Him to respond with deepest compassion, to participate with the sufferer in his or her grief. "Therefore, when Jesus saw her weeping, and the Jews who came with her weeping, He groaned in the spirit and was troubled. . . . Jesus wept" (John 11:33, 35).

Consider Job's Suffering

We cannot expect to know all the reasons for and understand completely the suffering we experience in our lifetime. Look at Job. "Have you considered My servant Job, that there is none like him on the earth, a blameless and upright man, one who fears God and shuns evil?" (Job 1:8). Job was a godly man who nevertheless experienced intense suffering, leaving him confused and bewildered. He was part of a cosmic battle between God and Satan. For a long time he struggled to make sense of his predicament, begging God to reveal the cause of his misfortune. Finally God spoke aloud to him. What He wanted from Job was his trust in whatever happened to him. He took pains to remind Job of His sovereignty and power.

Where were you when I laid the foundations of the
earth?
Tell Me, if you have understanding.
Who determined its measurements? . . .
To what were its foundations fastened,
Or who laid its cornerstone? . . .
Who then is able to stand against Me? . . .
Everything under heaven is Mine (Job 38:4–6;
41:10–11).

Job was never meant to know why he suffered. What
was important in the confrontation between God and Satan
was that even though Job did not understand, he still
trusted God.

God's words to Job were meant to remind him that
He was in control of Job's life no matter how wretched the
circumstances appeared. He was not cold and unfeeling
toward Job's suffering. On the contrary, He loved him and
felt concern for him is his deep agony. He had been
watching over Job throughout his long ordeal and cared
that he was broken, hurt, and confused.

Consider Our Suffering

The causes of our suffering may be too complex for
us to unravel, but we do know God is worthy of our trust
and He promises to be with us through our pain and
sorrow. "Be strong and of good courage; do not be afraid,
nor be dismayed, for the Lord your God is with you
wherever you go" (Josh. 1:9).

Never think when you suffer that you suffer alone,
that the Lord has placed you in a dreadful predicament and
then turned away or sat back, uncaring, to watch. No
matter what the adversity, no matter what God's reason,
you can know for a fact that He is not only absolutely
righteous but also benevolent, merciful, and loving toward
you. He is a tender sympathetic Father. "As a father pities
his children, So the Lord pities those who fear Him. For
He knows our frame; He remembers that we are dust" (Ps.
103:13–14).

Christians frequently take all this to mean that the
battered woman should do nothing to change her situation
or bring relief to herself. Patient endurance, they say,

demonstrates her trust in the Lord. Her suffering is from God and has the potential to bring about some good—to mature her, to teach her something even if it is only to endure patiently, or to exhibit her piety to an unbelieving world. Many think the Scripture urges her to surrender to her suffering without question, but this is not the case.

Biblical accounts of the lives of God's most faithful servants verify that there are many different ways to respond to difficult circumstances encountered in life. God does not require all His children to behave in precisely the same way. We must not box God in or attempt to regiment His actions or His wishes.

IS IT RIGHT TO TRY TO ESCAPE SUFFERING?

Many righteous men of the Bible endured terrible suffering. Abel was murdered by Cain. Job's family was killed, and his possessions were destroyed. Joseph was thrown into a pit and sold into slavery by his brothers. Paul had a physical ailment that tormented him to his dying day.

These men found themselves in situations from which they could not escape on their own and from which God chose not to deliver them supernaturally. Abel and Joseph were overpowered by their brothers, Job and Paul by natural disaster and disease. Their choice lay not in *whether* to endure but in *how* to endure. That is not to say they did not first do all they could to end their suffering. The Bible specifically records the efforts of Paul and Job to rid themselves of their burdens.

In the lives of other godly men, Scripture points out, God miraculously intervened to deliver His servants from harm. Daniel was saved from hungry lions; Shadrach, Meshach, and Abednego from burning to death in a furnace. Job, too, was eventually restored to health and prosperity. Peter was delivered from prison, once by an earthquake and once by an angel. These men were helpless to change their situations, but God chose to rescue them supernaturally.

These biblical heroes come first to mind in discussions of suffering, and from their stories people tend to conclude that a suffering individual is to do nothing on his own behalf but wait patiently to see whether or not God spares him. In thinking that way we ignore the most common means God employs to deliver His servants from danger—His use of an individual's own initiative and good sense.

Both the Old and New Testaments record instances of such actions by individuals. When their capture was imminent, the spies sent out by Joshua asked Rahab to hide and protect them, even though they knew the Lord had given His blessing to their mission (see Josh. 2:14). David ran away from Saul, and later from his son Absalom, when his life was threatened (see 1 Sam. 20; 2 Sam. 15). Paul, courageous preacher that he was, allowed himself to be lowered over the side of the city wall at Damascus in order to save his life (see Acts 9:25). Once he saved himself from a beating by reminding his guards that he was a Roman citizen and what they were about to do to him was illegal (see Acts 22). Many other times he *was* beaten, imprisoned, even stoned for his preaching. But when he had the chance, he preserved his life.

These men were not of lesser spiritual worth than others. The two spies were handpicked by Joshua from among thousands of Israelite soldiers. David was an outstanding poet, a strong and courageous leader, a military genius, a great king, and above all, a man "after God's own heart." Paul was an apostle, the author of more than a dozen books of the New Testament, a dedicated servant of the Lord who had a dramatic personal encounter with Jesus.

These men did not lack faith. The spies said, "Truly the LORD has delivered all the land into our hands" (Josh. 2:24). David wrote, "The LORD is my light and my salvation, whom shall I fear?" (Ps. 27:1). Paul wrote, "For to me, to live is Christ, and to die to gain" (Phil. 1:21).

They were not scolded or reproved by God for their actions. They were not reminded that they should have endured the suffering they faced and awaited God's possible miraculous intervention. God honored their responsible and prudent efforts to save themselves.

Whatever way deliverance from suffering comes, it is ultimately by God's hand. God is responsible for every rescue. "God is to us a God of deliverances; And to God the Lord belong escapes from death" (Ps. 68:20 NASB).

Consider David and Saul

The Bible record of the life of David offers a fairly detailed picture of an actual case of abuse, for this great servant of God and Israel's first king, Saul, were involved in a violent relationship. It may come as a surprise, but there are many parallels between David's relationship to Saul and the battered wife's relationship to her abusive husband. So many similarities exist that the scriptural accounts of the lives of the men deserve a closer look here.

King Saul exhibited numerous traits typical of abusive husbands. When he was anointed king of Israel, he was a promising young man, tall, handsome, and courageous. However, he soon demonstrated that he lacked self-control and felt uncertain and inadequate. He was plagued with emotional problems—insecurity, depression, and dependency. He was overly conscious of, and sensitive to, the opinions of others, and he was given to sudden paroxysms of anger. In this state of wild frenzy he twice threw his spear at David in an attempt to pin him to the wall. As the years went by, his harsh feelings intensified toward David; he became increasingly rebellious, egotistical, jealous, and abusive.

Occasionally he would seem to come to his senses, repent, and ask David's forgiveness, admitting that his hatred for the young man was irrational and promising thereafter to allow him to live in peace. "Then Saul said, 'I have sinned. Return, my son David. For I will harm you no more, because my life was precious in your eyes this day. Indeed I have played the fool and erred exceedingly'" (1 Sam. 26:21). But with time, his suspicions would reassert themselves, and his vows of repentance would be forgotten.

As Saul's life paralleled the abusive husband's, so many aspects of David's life were similar to those of a battered wife. He was a young man when he was first taken from his father's house to the king's court to be the royal musician. At first all went well. The king, though moody and unpredictable, loved David's music. In fact, David was so pleasing to Saul that he was kept always by the king's side. However, David's relationship with his monarch eventually began to crumble. Like the battered wife, David did nothing to deserve the ill-treatment he received. He was a loyal subject, an upstanding citizen, and no threat whatever to Saul. But he was betrayed, demoted, and finally attacked by the king. He was eventually forced to flee for his life. He told his friend Jonathan, "There is but a step between me and death" (1 Sam. 20:3).

Although David showed respect, love, and allegiance to his sovereign, even in the face of Saul's hatred and persecution, he was never able to curb the hostility Saul felt for him. David lived away from the court until Saul died.

David did three things in the face of his abuse. First, he confided in Jonathan. He talked his situation over with this one close friend. Second, he ran for his life even though it meant committing an act of treason. Third, he gave God the credit for his deliverance.

> Then David spoke to the LORD the words of this song, on the day when the LORD had delivered him from the hand of all his enemies, and from the hand of Saul. . . .
> "The LORD is my rock, my fortress and my deliverer;
> The God of my strength, in Him I will trust,
> My shield and the horn of my salvation,
> My stronghold and my refuge.
> My Savior, You save me from violence" (2 Sam. 22:1–3).

Notice what David did not do. He did not curse or condemn Saul. He did not seek revenge or become bitter even when his life was threatened. He did not wait around

136

for God to deliver him supernaturally. He did not consider that his flight from Saul was wrong. In all that he wrote about himself—and he wrote extensively—he never confessed his actions in fleeing Saul to be sin.

Did he do right? Does a battered wife do right to run from her husband when he is attacking her? The Bible offers no specific commendation to David for fleeing Saul. But we can infer that his actions pleased the Lord based on two Scripture selections.

Consider Jonathan

First Samuel 20:22 indicates that the godly Jonathan encouraged David to run away from Saul, when he told David, "Go your way, for the LORD has sent you away."

And years after David's flight, the Lord sent him this message through the prophet Nathan. "This is what the LORD, the God of Israel says: 'I anointed you king over Israel, and I delivered you from the hand of Saul' " (2 Sam. 12:7).

Consider Peter

Advocating a separation between spouses would seem, on the surface, to directly contradict the words of 1 Peter 3. Peter devotes the whole of this epistle to the subject of suffering, but the third chapter specifically addresses Christian women with nonbelieving husbands and tells them to do good without fear. Peter also speaks of suffering for the sake of the gospel. At first reading, it appears that he must have the battered woman in particular in mind. Is this really the case?

Apparently Peter was in Rome at the time he wrote this letter. Suffering along with other Christians under Nero's savage persecutions, he wrote to encourage and strengthen the Christians in Asia for the persecution he could see ahead for them.

Peter appealed to believers to watch their behavior in front of the Gentile population, to carefully obey the lawfully constituted authorities, and to live out their testimony as Christians by their exemplary behavior. He urged them to retain their commitment to the accepted social institutions of the day, even though these might be repressive. This included obedience to dictatorial autocrats and heathen slave owners. He had a twofold purpose for these requests. First, he wanted nothing to bring disrepute to the gospel (see 1 Peter 2:12, 15). Second, he didn't want them to have to endure any more suffering than was necessary (see 1 Peter 3:16–17). There was no need, in his mind, for Christians to flaunt deliberately the laws of the land or for Christian women to harangue openly their unbelieving husbands with the gospel message. These actions would only serve to add to the coming persecution. Peter urged them instead to witness by their behavior— wordlessly. His plea was for an exhibition of modesty, quietness, and gentleness, which would fulfill both aspects of his twofold request.

Consider Christians Today

How do Christians today best follow these directives to keep spotless the reputation of the gospel message and to minimize the amount of suffering believers must endure? By seeing that wife abuse is stopped. Assault is illegal whether it is one's employee, wife, child, friend, or a stranger who is beaten. In following Peter's counsel to obey the law, we must not let women continue to be assaulted in their own homes—especially in the name of Christianity. The practice of discouraging women from taking action to save themselves from abusive mates has already caused the church, and through it, Christ Himself, to be maligned, as this quote from a secular book on wife abuse shows:

> The clergy preaches a male-oriented theology and structure of the marriage relationship. The clergy has not been in the vanguard of help for the battered wife. Instead, its attitudes about woman's place, duty, and nature, have added to the problem.[1]

When a Christian is called on to suffer, according to Peter, he or she should suffer for the sake of righteousness, not for any improper conduct. He wrote, "But even if you

should suffer for righteousness' sake you are blessed"
(1 Peter 3:14). One who suffers for righteousness' sake
suffers because men hate Christ. The presence of Christ's
goodness in a believer causes men to hate and therefore
persecute him or her.

But the battered wife is not beaten because she is a
Christian. It is not her radiant Christian testimony that
causes her husband to lash out at her. In fact, one might
say it is not *her* at all. Abusive husbands batter their wives
because violence reduces tension and helps them feel in
control; because they have learned from childhood that
this is how conflict and stress are handled best; and
because they can get away with it. They batter because
nobody stops them.

It is not the wife's righteous behavior that causes her
husband to beat her. He beats her no matter how she
behaves. There have been some cases, certainly, where
husbands have used the excuse of their mates' faith to
abuse them. Yet these women have found that if they
discontinue church attendance, Bible study, and other
religious activities, their husbands find another excuse for
their attacks. It is simply the nature of the problem.

Does the battered Christian wife of the twentieth
century achieve any positive results in remaining in an
abusive relationship? Does the suffering bring about good
for her, her family, her neighbors? Does her behavior
result in her husband's conversion? Does she learn something from the experience, even if only endurance? Does
the non-Christian world marvel at her conduct and stand
convicted by her piety? Thousands of cases say no. The
longer the abused woman remains in an abusive situation,
the more deterioration there is in her partner's respect for
her and in her own self-esteem. Her husband increasingly
despises her weakness. His contempt for her and her faith
intensifies. Family counselors Howard Green and Cathy
Suttor report:

> Children in such situations initially support
> their mother, but after prolonged exposure to the
> violence and her failure to do anything about it,

they become disillusioned with her and often begin to side with the abusive father. Neighbors and friends, even professional counselors, who are initially supportive find it difficult to continue in that frame of mind if nothing is done to change the situation. If this woman is a Christian, she brings about the reverse of Peter's intended effort by remaining in an abusive situation. Rather than growing in its admiration and respect for her, the world begins at first to question and later to reject her for her lack of action. Ultimately, the battered woman grows to despise herself, attaining neither personal growth through discipline nor any effective witness to the non-Christian world.[2]

TO THE BATTERED CHRISTIAN WIFE:

If your husband abuses you, do not fear that this is a punishment from God or that it in any way reflects a divine disapproval of you. Do not be afraid to look for a way to end the abuse. You do not have to endure suffering for the rest of your life to benefit spiritually from the experience.

Don't expect continued acceptance of your husband's abusive behavior to some day bring him to his senses. The more you tolerate indignities and pain, the more he will administer them.

Take courage from the examples of men like Paul and David who made every effort to escape suffering and death whether by calling on their legal rights, running away and hiding, or depending on assistance from friends.

Remember that God is with you when you suffer, that He loves you and understands what you are going through.

"You who seek God, let your heart revive.
For the LORD hears the needy.
And does not despise His who are prisoners"
(Ps. 69:32–33 NASB).

140

7

What Can a Battered Wife Do?

"I have realized, finally, after all these years, that things are never going to get better on their own. I've been the best wife I can be, but the abuse is getting worse. I've got to do something, but I don't know where to begin. What can I do?"

ARE YOU A BATTERED WOMAN?

If you have read the preceding chapters, you will know whether or not your marriage bears a resemblance to the ones described there. You will, it is hoped, feel relieved to find you are not alone. Your situation is shared by thousands and thousands of others. Yet you may be reluctant to label yourself abused.

Many women find it difficult to admit. They think in doing so they place themselves in a category with all women who have "failed" at marriage, all those who somehow weren't "good enough." Their self-confidence is badly shaken by exposure to the prevailing attitude that battered women must deserve what they get. They deny or cover up their injuries for years, thinking they risk losing the respect of family and friends. Christian women have the additional burden of worrying about the reaction from the church.

But admitting you are abused is the first of several steps you must take if you are determined to change your life for the better. The next step involves confronting and dealing with the flood of emotions you have been trying to ignore or suppress for years.

Do you, on the one hand, find fury erupting like a volcano inside yourself when your husband hurts or degrades you? On the other hand, do you become nostalgic and sentimental when you remember the good times and the little gestures of affection that are so endearing in him? Between beatings do you stifle your resentment and fear and instead fantasize about his promises to change, to reform? Do you cling to the belief that a change for the better is just around the corner, only to find your hopes dashed when his vows are broken and his good intentions dissolve?

Acknowledge the fact that you are angry with him.

It is legitimate for you to feel this way. Ignoring anger or denying it will work against you. Christian counselor Norman Wright says, "Repressing anger is like placing a wastebasket full of paper in a closet and setting fire to it. The fire will either burn itself out, or it could set the entire house on fire and burn it down. The energy produced by anger cannot be destroyed. It must be converted or directed into another channel."[1]

Take steps to end the abuse in your relationship.

Ephesians 4:26 exhorts, "Be angry, and do not sin." You need to get angry to get moving, but you should keep it under control. Take advantage of the stimulation it provides; use it to get yourself actively involved in pursuing a change in your lifestyle, and then let it go. Do not carry it as a burden for the rest of your life. Anger must not be allowed to grow into bitterness or a preoccupation with revenge. "Beloved, do not avenge yourselves, but rather give place to wrath; for is is written, 'Vengeance is Mine, I will repay,' says the Lord" (Rom. 12:19).

Chaplain Wesley Monfalcone warns, "Desire for revenge is self-defeating. It eats away like an untreated cancer which gradually destroys all your vitality."[2] Bitterness will leave you all empty inside, exhausted and shriveled up. It will leave its mark on your face, your personality, and all your future relationships.

Are you afraid? When your husband is at work, do you dread his coming home? When he is home, do you walk on eggs, watching him closely to gauge his mood, ready at a moment's notice to do anything to pacify him? Are you a hostage in your own house?

You may fear life *with* your husband, but that may not be your only fear. You may also fear life *without* him. *How would I manage emotionally and financially without him?* you ask yourself. *Would I be able to raise the children alone? Would he try to take them away from me? Could he come after me and harm me?* Certainly many of these fears are well-founded. Part of the goal of this chapter is to help take away fear, to suggest ways and means of dealing with it or overcoming it, and to assist you in discovering where to go for the support and encouragement you will need to function in spite of it.

Are you ashamed? It is common for abused women to feel that the trouble in their marriage is somehow all their fault. They believe their family's emotional well-being depends solely on them and they are responsible for anything that goes wrong. If you wonder whether something is the matter with you that you cannot make a success of your role as wife, rest assured this is not the case. People who study wife abuse affirm that your husband has the problem, not you. It may be difficult to hold that thought when you are so used to hearing that *you* are worthless, *you* are inadequate, *you* are incapable, but it is true. You have not failed, and you need not feel guilt or shame that your marriage is in trouble.

Possibly the most destructive emotion you may be experiencing is hopelessness. You seem to have no options, to be trapped in an unalterable predicament. You live an isolated life, with few friends to lean on or to run to for support, and you think yourself too weak to do anything on your own. You see yourself as powerless, a little pebble on the beach, totally at the mercy of the tide that moves you from place to place. It is especially likely you are feeling this way if you have tried before to break out of the cycle of violence and have failed.

You may have tried any or all the traditional sources of help—family, friends, doctor, pastor, even the police— and come away empty-handed. As a result you feel total despair. You may be wondering why you are even reading this book. After all, it has been proved to you time and time again that you are in prison physically, emotionally, financially, and legally. You may see your faith as a part of the prison wall surrounding you.

It's okay. These feelings are shared by most battered

women. Don't let them stand in your way or prevent your taking appropriate action to help your mate, your children, and yourself.

HOW TO HELP YOUR MATE

"I don't understand my life, why the Lord has put me in this situation or what He has in store for me. But I do know that things don't happen by accident. I am in this place for a purpose. I really love Mike, and I feel that since the Lord put me here He wants me to help him. If I run out on my husband, who will be left to help him? I'll be thwarting God's plans."

Many Christian women who are abused understandably feel that they are responsible for helping their husbands to reform. Certainly at some level this is true. They are in a partnership ordained by God, and He has said that marital partnership is permanent. He has also told us that as Christians we are responsible for encouraging the spiritual growth of one another (see Eph. 4:11–13) and the salvation of the lost (see Matt. 28:19–20).

The mistake these women make is in assuming that putting up with abusive behavior will ultimately cause their husbands to see the error of their ways and become loving, considerate spouses. That is not the case.

"If stripping oneself of dignity would preserve a marriage, I would enthusiastically endorse it. Unfortunately, the opposite is true," says James Dobson in discussing the problem of failing marriages. "Attempts by one side to 'buy off' an aggressor or offender appear to represent peace proposals, but they merely precipitate further insult and conflict."[3]

Helping your husband does not mean accepting his abuse. In fact, it means exactly the reverse. In some ways it is easier to simply continue to allow yourself to be mistreated. Initiating change can be frightening, but don't deceive yourself that further martyrdom will eventually bring your mate to a shocked realization of his wrongdoing.

On the contrary, your compliance only reinforces his abusive behavior. Investigative journalists Roger Langley and Richard C. Levy note:

> Studies show that marital violence tends to escalate. The battered woman who hopes "things will get better" without taking some action is betting long odds against herself. A woman who wants to change her life has to become convinced that the change will come only if she takes action. . . . The critical point for a battered woman to remember is that it is up to her to initiate the action that will end her abuse. It seldom works the other way around.[4]

It is essential for you to remember, however, that nothing you can do will force your partner to reform. He is responsible for his own behavior. He chooses to act as he does. His cruelty is not your fault. It is not in your power to change him. But you can change yourself, the way you react to him, and the rules of the relationship.

How to Deal with Nonphysical Abuse

If you are a psychologically or emotionally abused woman, the best way for you to help your husband is to stop being his victim. This means altering the way you think, feel, and act. It is not easy. You start by reaffirming your dignity as a person of value. If you are like most people who have been repeatedly mistreated, intimidated, and ground down, your self-esteem has taken quite a beating. Until you regain a solid sense of self-respect and self-acceptance, you'll remain trapped. So your first task boils down to this: You need to learn to like yourself again. And you can.

PAY ATTENTION TO YOURSELF

One way to work on this area of your life is to begin showing yourself some consideration. Act as if you like yourself and little by little you'll begin to actually feel it. Pay attention to your health and well-being. Do what you can to look your best every day. Put on makeup. Keep your clothes clean and in good repair. Treat yourself as well as you treat other members of the family. Prepare yourself a favorite meal. Buy yourself a present. Indulge yourself in an occasional bubble bath or trip to the movies. You are a worthwhile person and caring for yourself will help confirm this in your own mind.

Does it seem selfish? It's not. Jesus told us to love others as we love ourselves. Your returning self-confidence will benefit your children and your spouse as it benefits you.

Does recapturing lost self-respect seem too high a goal for the tiny bit of energy you possess? Then find additional power outside yourself. There is one sure source of healthy self-confidence, strength, and peace in the midst of humiliation, helplessness, and chaos. It is the tender and unconditional love of Christ. Don't be afraid to look to heaven for a reappraisal of your worth and dignity. Become involved in personal or small group Bible study. As you see how highly Jesus values you, you can learn to value yourself.

BUILD A SUPPORT TEAM FOR YOURSELF

Another effective source of affirmation is family and friends. Have you been cut off from their support and encouragement? Reestablish your ties with them. Phone, write, visit. Begin to rebuild relationships which can serve as a support system. This will be very helpful in the months to come.

Getting back your self-esteem is absolutely essential if you are going to take action to help your husband. That new personal strength will enable you to break out of old patterns of behavior and establish new ones.

You and your spouse have been following a well-defined script for years. The dialogue between you has been learned and learned well. He blames you and you accept it. He scolds you and you feel shame. He humiliates you and you apologize. These are the automatic reflex responses your relationship demands. Now that must change. You stop playing the role of the inept, utterly independent wife. You break away from the old habits and begin to respond differently. You require his respect.

This second step toward ending your career as your partner's victim presents a hefty challenge. It will be a totally new experience for you to set limits on his behavior. But it is essential. Decide how you wish to be treated and what behaviors you will no longer accept.

Holding your ground without being hostile may be the most helpful and loving thing you can do for him. Love, after all, is more than accepting him the way he is. It is also wanting him to be all God created him to be.

If the prospect seems overwhelming, maybe even wrong, understand this. Your confrontations are not assaults on him. Rather, they are defenses of yourself. You don't argue. You don't try to justify yourself. You don't attack or belittle him. But you do respond to his abuse calmly and firmly. "I will not stand here and be shouted at," you say. Or, "I am not going to intimidated by you," or, "I don't want you to talk to me in that way."

As difficult as this is to do and as impossible as it may sound as you read it, it is the recommended strategy for dealing with nonphysical abuse. It accomplishes something very important because it makes it very uncomfortable for your mate to abuse you. It tells him what he is doing is no longer acceptable.

In the weeks and months ahead, you must maintain this confrontive posture with him without backing down. Moreover, it is important that you begin making decisions and exerting your independence again. Start small, but start. These skills may be rusty if you have been in an abusive relationship for long. You need to get used to exercising those mental muscles with which you make judgments and choices. Count even your smallest efforts a success.

Right from the start your new behavior will throw your partner's life into chaos. He will do anything he can to restore the old order of things. More than anything he will want you to abandon the strength and confidence you show. He's an expert at intimidation and well versed in tactics which throw you off balance and subdue you. Expect his opposition.

He may yell, call you crazy, coldly insult you, bully, sulk, withdraw, or threaten you. He may break down and weep, plead for mercy, and appear so abject and remorseful that you are tempted to back off. But if you persevere, over the next weeks and months, your tactics will begin to have an effect. For one thing, you'll grow stronger. And you'll feel better about yourself. You'll discover you are okay even if he doesn't think so and you can go on with your life.

"It was terrifying to stand up for myself," one woman said to her counselor. "I'd rather have run away. But I also felt like an animal who'd been caught in a trap then suddenly let go by accident. I was frightened, sure. But it wasn't the same fear as before. It was fear and delicious anticipation mixed together. I was free."

This is a long process and, of course, no one can predict how your spouse will handle it over the course of time. He may choose to change along with you and work to restore your marriage. That will be a wonderful outcome. Or, as he gains a grudging admiration for you, he may at least back off from his abusive behavior, even if he goes no further than that. Or, he may decide to try physical violence to retain his control over you. The possibility of this should keep you on guard, watching for danger signs and ready to get out if necessary. Do not put your life or the lives of your children at risk by staying in the house with a physically abusive husband. And do not feel guilty if the situation deteriorates in this way. It is the recognized pattern that nonphysical abuse progresses to physical abuse with time.

What has been described here, in brief, is an immensely simplified overview of difficult and long-term work, work best accomplished with the guidance of a professional counselor. A counselor understands what you are going through, can help you see what's real when your spouse confuses you, offers comfort in times of emotional pain, and can coach you as you work at regaining control of your life. Suggestions for finding such a person are listed later in this chapter.

How to Deal with Physical Abuse

Loving your husband, and knowing he needs help, means you must first of all allow him to face the unpleasant consequences of his actions. Rather than constantly covering up for him, you must permit him to encounter public scorn, the disillusionment of his children, and the disgust of his friends. Assaulting you is a crime, a felony, and obviously a grievous sin in the eyes of the Christian community; you may have to let the authorities arrest him.

In a sixteen-month study conducted by the Minneapolis police, officers randomly responded to 250 cases of domestic assault by either mediating between the spouses, arresting the husband, or banishing him from the house for at least eight hours. As a result of that experiment Minneapolis Chief of Police Anthony Bouza gave this advice to abused wives: "I have asked the women of our city who are repeatedly beaten by their spouses to step forward and press charges so that my officers can arrest their offending partners. Arrest seems to be the best way of deterring domestic violence."[5]

Beyond calling the police, how do you let him know you will not tolerate abuse any longer? How do you awaken him, once and for all, to the seriousness of the situation? Talking to him won't do it. Nor will fighting back. What else is there?

SEPARATE FROM YOUR HUSBAND

So far, separation has proved to be the best method of getting husbands to realize they need help, says author Jennifer Baker Fleming, founder and director of The Women's Resource Network.

> It is usually necessary for the battered wife to put distance between herself and her husband in order to stop the abuse. . . . If your husband is

151

unwilling to get help, it will probably be necessary for you to leave at some point. We remind you again that the abuse will not go away by itself. In fact, it will get worse.[6]

"The women should take a stand. They should say, 'I will leave,' or 'I will go to a shelter, or go home, or whatever.' The women should threaten and make it stick. The women's shelter here in Bloomington [Indiana] is the best thing that ever happened for me and my success with abusive men,"[7] states clinical psychologist Laurence Barnhill.

Even the Christian community is acknowledging the necessity of this approach. Esther Lee Olson, a Christian psychologist who works with battered women, writes, "The only way you can help your husband is by forcing him to recognize the serious consequences of what he has done. Ironically, it may take the threat of divorce to bring him to this point."[8]

The consensus is clear.

Separation has the following advantages:

1. For the husband, separation provides the stimulus to acknowledge his abusive behavior and look for a way to help himself overcome his aggressive outbursts. It is a clear signal from his wife. It effectively prevents his committing further illegal acts against her.

2. For the wife, separation provides physical safety and a chance to recuperate from injuries. It also gives her an opportunity to seek counseling.

3. For the children, separation provides relief from the terrible strain of living in terror, wondering if one parent is going to kill the other.

The decision to take this step is not an easy one for any woman. It may take months or years before you reach the point where you feel separation is appropriate for you.

If and when you decide to go, where will it be? For each one of you the answer will be different. Look first to your own resources. Can you go home to your parents temporarily? Do they understand and sympathize with you? Can you count on them? What about other relatives?

Your sister? Your aunt? One caution should be mentioned here. When you ask family members to shelter you, your husband will have no trouble locating you. If you feel it would not be safe for him to know where you are, staying with a relative is risky. There is also the possibility that your stay might put your family in jeopardy. Bonnie's husband found her at her parents' home, grabbed her little brother, and held him at knife point until Bonnie agreed to go home with him. Staying with a friend is another option with the same drawbacks.

As the Christian community becomes more aware of the desperate predicament of abused wives, it is hoped churches will open their doors to provide shelter for those who hurt. Do not overlook this possibility when you are exploring where to go. Lucille Travis, reporting on wife abuse in *Eternity* magazine, told of an abused woman whose pastor took her into his home and protected her with his life.[9]

A shelter specializing in helping battered women is perhaps the best alternative, although there are some disadvantages. Such a shelter is bound to be noisy and crowded. There may be no room available on the day you wish to enter, and some shelters have long waiting lists. A limit on how long you can stay will be in effect. Staff members may have a counseling bias toward divorce. Nevertheless a shelter offers good protection, counseling by professionals, and a chance to talk with other women who have had a life similar to yours. You'll be respected, cared about, and understood. A few shelters now offer a program for husbands, too, but this aspect of domestic violence counseling is still quite new.

TAKE RESPONSIBILITY FOR YOURSELF

You can and should do some things for yourself, regardless of what you decide to do about your husband. It is important that you begin early to take hold of the reins and assume more responsibility for what happens to you. For some of you this will be more difficult than for others. Read through the following suggestions. Certain ones will be right for you, and others won't fit your situation. You will have to decide which you will follow and which you cannot. Any that involve your safety or that of your children should receive your first attention.

Safeguard Your Spiritual Health

Esther Lee Olson says Christian women have special problems because of their background and beliefs and those of people around them. But they also have special comfort and solace. "For God is real and He holds those who suffer close to His heart. . . . It is in Christ that we find deliverance, all of us—the poor, the lonely, the brokenhearted, the abused. We find shelter in Christ."[10]

He understands because He went through it all Himself. Did you ever consider what kind of experience Jesus had on earth? He knew what it was like to be lonely (Mark 15:34), overwhelmed with grief (Matt. 26:38), powerless (Isa. 53:7), humiliated (Luke 22:63), betrayed by a trusted companion (Matt. 26:48), abandoned by His friends (Matt. 26:56), falsely accused (Luke 11:15), jeered at and taunted (Matt. 27:40), despised and rejected (Isa. 53:3), spit on (Mark 14:65), slapped and beaten (John 19:1, 3), robbed of his clothes (John 19:23), and tortured to death (Mark 15:20). He knows how difficult your life is. There is nothing you can face that He hasn't faced before you. "Come to Me, all you who are weary and burdened," He says, "and I will give you rest" (Matt. 11:28). He knows you through and through, every weakness, every strength, every sorrow, every joy. His knowledge is more than intellectual. It is warm, personal, compassionate, and full of His love.

Saturate yourself with the Word. Study it daily. Read and reread it. Memorize the psalms that bring you the most comfort. Learn what the Lord has to say to the oppressed. Find out how the Scriptures relate to wife abuse. Be ready to explain your position to others who may ask you. Drink in the refreshment the Bible holds out to you. Make it your foundation and your security.

Terry Davidson, a secular writer, recommends this

for all abused women who plan to stay in their marriages: "Immerse yourself in the dogma that sustains you." She says, "Ambivalence is an uncomfortable state to remain in. If you really feel beyond self-help or you are committed by your religion or other strong pulls to the marriage you've got, then you may as well devote yourself to the philosophy that created it. Give a lot of thought to it. Let it fill all your time between assaults."[11]

Pray. Olson calls communication with God the most vital responsibility for the battered Christian woman. But do not limit your prayers to repeated requests for miraculous divine intervention. Use prayer to deepen your knowledge of, and trust in, the Lord. Worship Him. Adore Him. Review aloud His attributes: His holiness, His mercy, His justice, and His love. Pray for strength; pray for wisdom. Pray for your husband and your children. Pray the prayers of David, which are recorded in the Psalms. David's prayers reflect his frequent need for deliverance, but they always end on a note of thanksgiving and praise for God's lovingkindness and goodness. Ask God to take charge of your life, and don't let that stop you from doing what you know you can.

Safeguard Your Emotional Health

One universal piece of advice pervades the literature on wife abuse and frequently crops up in interviews with battered women and those who help them. It is this: Share what you are going through with someone else. Tell someone you trust what is happening. A feeling of isolation and loneliness may be the biggest barrier you face in coping with your situation. Don't allow it to get the better of you. Turn to others—or even to one other person who believes in you and sympathizes with you. As one battered woman expressed it, "You have to have people to lean on. You feel so bad about yourself that you can't do anything alone."[12] If the people you choose to confide in are sympathetic but have trouble grasping the seriousness of your situation, get them to read some of the literature on domestic violence.

Whatever it takes, find someone who will listen and give you moral support. Try family members, church friends, neighbors. If possible, make new friends by getting involved in activities outside your home. Take a night school course in a subject that interests you and get to know your classmates. Join a women's Bible study or other small group that meets in or near your neighborhood. One word of caution—be discreet. One desperate woman who confided in *all* her friends and neighbors was regarded by them as merely an attention-seeker.

If your husband has restricted your freedom to the extent that you feel you cannot join an activity in the community, at least get out and meet your neighbors. You need outside support. Even if you have to do this without your husband's knowledge, do it. It is essential that you have others to help you.

Find yourself a counselor. A good therapist can work with you and your situation in a knowledgeable way, can help you sort out what you should do and when, and can give you the kind of advice friends are not equipped to give. Going to a counselor will not be possible for all of you. Some of you have husbands who won't allow it. Some of you can't afford it. For many of you there will be no such help within a reasonable distance. All these obstacles are real, and some, perhaps, are insurmountable. However, if you are in a position to seek professional help, by all means take advantage of it. Certain words of caution are necessary here, too. You must carefully screen the person in whom you plan to place your trust.

Who is the right counselor, you may ask yourself. Here are some areas to consider in choosing the right counselor.

1. **Is the counselor a Christian?** Battered Christian women have a particular point of view and philosophy of life that may not be understood or supported by a secular therapist. You'll feel better working with someone who you know understands your position and will be giving advice in keeping with your faith.

2. **Is the counselor experienced in the area of domestic**

violence? The importance of this cannot be overstated. This person will demonstrate an attitude of support for you. Counselors familiar with the dynamics of family violence will not give credence to the various stereotyped myths surrounding battered wives. They will know the community support systems well enough to get you whatever assistance you need and will be at your side if you need an advocate to deal with bureaucratic red tape.

Ask prospective counselors whether they have worked with domestic violence cases. Ask if they have read the available literature. Any therapist who has not kept current with the literature on family violence, or who has never had a client with your problem, is probably not for you. Find someone experienced in the field. The number is growing.

If you absolutely cannot find anyone who has had experience with wife abuse, you may have to settle for someone without experience. But test that person's point of view before making any commitment. Outline your story, and watch for a reaction that shows immediate recognition of the danger you are in and willingness to help make arrangements for your safety.

3. **Is the counselor tolerant of your anger?** Will he or she allow you the time you need to pour out the horror, the fears, and the frustrations of your life?

4. **Will the counselor let you make your own decisions?** The right counselor will give support but will leave with you the right to decide to stay with your husband or leave, reconcile or divorce.

The counselors who should be avoided can be identified by the following characteristics:

> They believe that women are innately inferior and provoke, enjoy, or deserve the abuse they receive.
>
> They imply or tell you outright that you are to blame for what is happening to you; they do not believe you; or they think you are exaggerating.
>
> They make you feel guilty.

157

They offer to help you endure the suffering but do not present concrete suggestions for changing the status quo.

They tell you it is sinful or wrong to feel angry.

They will not see you and your husband separately because they have the philosophy that it takes two to fight. They place equal blame on both parties.

They do not insist on, as a first consideration, the stopping of all abuse when working with you and your husband together.

Prospective counselors may have multiple degrees and years in practice, but there is no guarantee that their services will meet your needs. Wife abuse is becoming more widely publicized these days, so the chances of finding a therapist who understands the problem grow greater with time. However, the number of qualified Christian counselors available is still small.

If you have no idea where to find a counselor, try calling a crisis hot line or rape hot line and explaining your situation over the phone. Or ask your pastor to recommend a counseling agency.

Find out all you can about wife abuse. Read the books in your library on the subject. Watch for magazine articles, and be alert to radio talk shows where experts discuss it. Educate yourself. You'll feel less isolated and disgusted with yourself when you find out how many others share your situation. Learn what to expect from your battering mate. Learn the cycle, the usual pattern. You'll no longer be taken in by empty promises to reform. You'll be more aware of what can happen and be ready for it. You will be forewarned that wife beating, unchecked, gets worse and worse. Suggestions for handling battering incidents and lists of possible sources of help will prepare you for the future, for making realistic and wise decisions about seeking assistance.

Stop trying to be a "better" wife. At some point, you are going to have to come to terms with the fact that you will never get your husband to stop beating you by being perfect. For years you may have been telling yourself that if you just try harder, you will make him happy at last, and his brutality will cease.

Chaer Roberts, co-founder of the Denver-based AMEND (Abusive Men Exploring New Directions), says, "A lot of women think that if they can stop 'irritating' the men they'll stop battering. That's not true. The men have to change."[13]

Concede that you will never do enough to please him. There will always be something he can use to justify getting angry and hurting you. Stop spending all your energy trying to please a man who will never be satisfied. Pursuing such an unattainable goal will wear you down. Instead, concentrate some effort where it will do the most good. Devote your energy to the rest of your family. They need you.

Begin to take some steps toward independence. Learn how to make use of public transportation, for example. Study bus routes and timetables until you feel confident traveling without relying on your husband to take you where you need to go. Because he can take away your car keys or disable your car, don't depend on driving. You'll be surprised at the new feeling of freedom it gives you to know that you can go somewhere by yourself if you need to.

Brush up on old job skills or learn new ones. Consider taking training in an area that will give you a marketable knowledge.

Set aside time each day for your own use, no matter how short it is—even fifteen minutes. Learn something new. Develop an interest in a subject you know nothing about. The library is a wonderful resource. It contains books on everything you might want to learn. Read up on the use of a metal detector, the rules of tennis, the history of the circus—anything. Teach yourself how to oil paint, repair appliances, garden organically. Battered women testify to the merit of this diversional therapy.

SAFEGUARD YOUR PHYSICAL HEALTH

A lot in your life depends on your keeping fit. You'll cope better, feel better, think more clearly, and look better if you work at maintaining your physical health.

Being beaten is hard on the body. Frequent beatings have a compound effect. The more you are beaten, the harder your body has to work to restore itself. Healing cannot take place without proper nutrition.

A well-balanced diet can be attained through good, commonsense eating, but you will probably need more than that to keep your body at its best. You will need extra protein to replace and repair tissues damaged during your husband's attacks on you. Meats, cheeses, milk, and fish are good sources of protein, but less expensive sources— eggs, dried peas and beans, and peanut butter—are available. There are high protein foods to match every budget.

You will also benefit from additional vitamin C, which enhances the body's ability to heal itself. It can be taken in tablet form and is found in all vegetables and fruits, especially citrus fruits.

Try your best to avoid eating junk food, candy, potato chips, and other "empty calorie" snacks. Besides being expensive, they do not contribute to good nutrition and take away your appetite for more nourishing foods.

Appetite may be a problem for you. Some battered women feel too fearful and depressed to want to eat. Others find that the pain from an injured mouth or jaw diminishes their appetite. Remember that your children need you, and they need you healthy and alert and able to function in a crisis. You stand the best chance of being all these things if you make a point of eating and eating correctly.

Exercise is a second important way to safeguard your physical health. You may be exhausted and run down. If you are regularly beaten, your body devotes so much of its available energy to putting you back together that there may not be much left over for voluntary exertion. Beyond that, your state of mind may be such that your only wish is to be left alone to sleep.

But you do need some exercise every day. You cannot help but benefit from it. It will make you feel better physically, and it will probably lift your spirits, too. Try to get out into the fresh air for a short time daily. There are ways to work around restrictions your husband might have imposed on you. You may be able to walk around the block while he is at work. If he is home, you may use the excuse of escorting the children to and from school or running to the corner store for milk. Use your imagination to devise a way to get outside for a few minutes of brisk walking. If all else fails, exercise for a few minutes indoors. This isn't a substitute for being outside, but it will help tone your muscles and get your blood circulating. Increased agility is a benefit of exercise that should not be taken lightly. You never know when the ability to dodge a punch or a kick, or run away from a fist, might save your life.

Always seek medical attention for yourself after you have been beaten. Sometimes serious injuries occur: broken bones that require setting or lacerations that require suturing. You may sustain internal injuries that are not obvious to you immediately but that could prove fatal if not treated. Besides the treatment you receive at the doctor's office or hospital emergency room, medical assistance provides another valuable service—documentation of your injuries. Whether or not you are presently considering leaving your husband, it may happen that at some time in the future a separation might be imperative to save your life. In order to establish that you are not making up a history of abuse, should it come down to a court battle over custody of the children, for instance, it is essential that you have documented evidence to present in court. Be sure that you do not lie to medical personnel about the source of your injuries. In this case, it is most inappropriate for you to cover up for your husband. It won't do him any good in the long run to get away with hurting you, and it certainly won't do you any good, either.

DEVELOP A PLAN FOR HANDLING
BATTERING INCIDENTS

If you are a battered woman living with your husband, no matter where you are in the battering cycle, you face the certainty of another violent episode some time in the future. There is little chance of avoiding it unless you leave.

It is a good idea to make plans for what you will do the next time your husband beats you. You can think more clearly now than when you are being hurt. The following survival tactics have been collected from many sources and represent the best advice of victims and counselors alike.

Before an attack think about what you have been through already, and then decide what it will take to make you leave your husband. Be specific; write it down somewhere. Most importantly, stick to it. Will it be a death threat? An attack on the children? You will not be in any frame of mind to make rational decisions during an attack, so make up your mind now.

Expect your situation to worsen. Don't kid yourself that everything is going to be fine soon. Be realistic enough to recognize that each episode of abuse will probably be more severe than the last. Figure out where you can go to escape—a friend's house, a relative's, your church, a shelter. Then figure out how you will get there. Will you be able to drive? Should you take the bus? Is a neighbor willing to take you there?

Begin now to attach less importance to your belongings. There may come a time when you have to leave them behind. Many battered women find it hard to leave a battering situation even when they are in danger because they cannot bear to lose their material possessions. If you leave, there is every chance that you will have to make do with fewer of the nice things you now have. Remember that your life is more important than the things you own. Begin letting go now. "Watch out! Be on your guard against all kinds of greed; a man's life does not consist in the abundance of his possessions" (Luke 12:15 NIV).

Check out your home for a possible emergency refuge.
Is there a room you can lock yourself into? Some place
where you could run and be safe? If you find such a place,
head for it the minute you see the violence coming.

**Have a small bundle of essential items hidden in a
stash that you can retrieve if necessary.** It might be safe in
your home, or you may feel better asking a friend to keep it
for you. Include in it an extra set of car keys, important
documents—identification papers, health insurance infor-
mation, birth certificates—any medication you and the
children might need, an extra pair of glasses, disposable
diapers, extra clothes, and whatever money you can set
aside.

**To prevent serious disaster, consider leaving BEFORE
the inevitable explosion.** It you sense the tension is rising to
the point where an outburst is imminent, don't sit around
terrified and helpless. Get out while your husband is at
work. Leave a letter behind, explaining that you are afraid
and that you have decided for both your sakes it would be
better if you stayed away until things cool down. *Do not
tell him where you are.* Leave a copy of the letter with a
friend in case you need to verify your behavior later in
court.

**In the event you simply cannot leave, invite a friend or
relative to stay at your home with you for a while.** Abusive
husbands are usually reluctant to beat their wives in the
presence of outsiders. Remember, however, that the longer
this person stays, the less inhibiting his or her presence will
be to your husband. Do not be lulled into a false sense of
safety during the visit. Use the time you gain to make some
alternate plans.

**Do not feel uncomfortable making these arrangements
behind your husband's back.** Their purpose is to protect
your life and to give you a chance to do something that
could ultimately benefit him, too.

**During an attack, whenever your physical safety or
that of your children is threatened, get out immediately.**
There is the very real danger that serious physical damage
might be done you—you might even be murdered. Your

husband may try to intimidate you by telling you that if you leave, he will find and kill you. Without minimizing this possibility, consider that you make yourself even more vulnerable by staying.

If it is at all possible, take your children with you when you go. You will want to be sure they are protected and safe. Leaving the children behind gives your husband the chance to label you a bad mother for "abandoning" them. He may lure you back with reminders that they need you, and he may threaten to sue for legal custody on the grounds of desertion.

During an attack, it will be important for you not to panic or lash out at your spouse in anger. Keep as cool a head as you can. One of the two of you must be in control to minimize the destruction and injury. Do not try to talk your husband out of his violent mood. Do not argue with him. Anything you say may inflame him further. Keep out of his reach as long as you can. When you are being beaten, make special efforts to protect your head and abdomen.

Try to keep yourself from being cornered. Run outside, scream, and make as much noise as possible. Shout for the neighbors to call the police. Don't be embarrassed to have people watching your distress. They may be able to help you or serve as witnesses for you later.

If you can, call the police yourself. Your husband has no legal right to beat you. Don't be surprised if you find yourself being a bit intimidated by the police when they arrive. It may be against the law to assault another person, but police officers often see domestic disputes in a different light. They may want to do nothing more than to suggest that the two of you kiss and make up. If you are afraid to be left alone with your husband, ask the police to stay until you can pack a few things and leave. If you wish to have your husband arrested, be very firm about your request. If you don't get the help you need, take down the officers' names and badge numbers and report them to their superior.

Is it wiser to fight back or not to fight back? Some

counselors who work with battered women suggest that their clients seek out training in self-defense or one of the martial arts. They feel that a knowledge of "street fighting" or karate, for instance, not only helps a woman protect herself and gives her a new sense of self-confidence but might also halt her husband's attack, because for the first time she takes "an active stand against her fate" and stands up for herself.[14]

Others are not inclined to recommend this for two reasons. First, it forces the woman to stoop to her husband's level of interaction and compounds the violence in the home. If we say we abhor family violence, what business do we have recommending its use? Second, it is dangerous. The woman's attempts to fight back may backfire, enraging him more and resulting in worse injuries. Should she attempt to frighten him or keep him at bay with a weapon, he might wrench it from her grasp and use it against her instead. Or she might end up killing him.

After an attack get to a doctor. Have your injuries treated and documented. Do not lie about how you got the bruises and lacerations.

As much as you might want to forget the whole thing and pretend it never happened, save the torn and bloody clothing you wore during the fight. Have someone take color pictures of your injuries and keep them somewhere safe. You may need verification of what your husband has done to you.

Some battered women feel that it is best to stay through a beating, protecting themselves as best they can, but not running away. They think that if the woman can manage it, she is better off to wait until the next day to make her escape. While her husband is at work she can take the time she needs to gather her things together carefully and pack. There is less likelihood she will forget important items, and there is less chance her husband will follow her when she leaves, as he might have the night before.

Whenever it works out best for you to leave, do so, and STAY away until your husband gets help. You probably will feel strange and lonely, and you may not get the sympathy you expect. Your children may want to go back home, and your husband will try to get you to return with threats ("I'll find you and kill you"), promises ("I don't know what got into me, but it will never happen again"), or ultimatums ("Either you come home right now or don't bother to come home at all—I'm not waiting around forever"). Abusive husbands employ standard tactics to get their wives back.

You may find it difficult to stick to your decision. Many women who finally find the courage to leave end up going back home almost immediately. It is not uncommon for battered women to leave several times before they realize they must stay away until real change takes place in the relationship. *Withstand the urge to return until your husband demonstrates his repentance by attending counseling sessions.* This firmness on your part is extremely important.

> Thousands of case histories have proved that if a wife returns immediately, or even shortly after his begging or demanding, the violent patterns will not change and may even get worse. The wife beater sees how thoroughly he controls her, with no effort on his part. He sees her as stupid, masochistic, needing to be taken in hand. She embarrassed him; inconvenienced him. She deserves to be punished. Every dangerous thought he had before is reinforced.[15]

Your determination not to return until your husband receives counseling provides the most incentive for battering husbands to come for help. By staying away until he gets help, you force him to come to terms with the fact that the relationship is not going well, that the interaction between you is inappropriate, intolerable, unhealthy, and unchristian.

HELP YOUR CHILDREN

Earlier in this book, the destructive effect of domestic violence on children was discussed in detail. Now we need to focus on what can be done to minimize the trauma and stress for youngsters.

Spend time praying with and for your children. Bring them before the Lord and ask His special protection for them. Jesus' love for children is obvious in Scripture. We are told that whoever harms a child is destined for severe punishment (see Matt. 18:6) and that children's angels have special access to God the Father (see Matt. 18:10).

Let your children see your faith at work in your life. Share with them as you learn and grow spiritually. Allow them to see your dependence on the Lord for your every need. Memorize Psalm 121 together and recite it aloud with them when you are afraid.

Teach your children Bible truths; read to them from the Word. Acquaint them with heroes of the Old and New Testaments. They need role models for adulthood who exhibit godly character.

Give your children explicit instructions on what they are to do when you are being abused. You may want them to run to a neighbor's house for shelter. You may want them to call the police. You may want them to race to the bathroom and lock themselves in.

If it is possible, get them to safety when you suspect an attack is coming. Make arrangements for them to stay with a willing family member or nearby friend.

Above all, explain clearly and openly to them that they MUST NOT intervene between you and your husband because they might be seriously injured, intentionally or unintentionally. There is the possibility that, like Beth's children, they may want to come to your rescue in a fight but may be afraid to. If they feel they should protect you but cannot bring themselves to do so out of fear, the ensuing emotional conflict will produce an agony of guilt feelings later.

Guard your children against kidnapping. If you decide to separate from your husband, beware of the possibility of his kidnapping the children. Make sure they have adequate supervision at all times, that they are accompanied to and from school or day-care centers, that they are not left with anyone whose loyalty to you is suspect. Keeping school authorities informed of your situation might be helpful, but teachers and administrators, though sympathetic to you, might be legally unable to interfere with a father "picking up" his children. Kidnapping is a ploy a husband uses to punish his wife, to maintain control over her, or to force her to come back to him. It is a very real danger and should not be ignored.

There is no doubt that, whether or not they are physically abused, children in violent families suffer deep and lasting emotional effects from witnessing their father's cruelty to their mother. Never deceive yourself that your children are unaware of, or unconcerned about, the severe conflict in your family. Children in violent families are afraid. They feel vulnerable whether or not they show it. They feel guilty being angry with their father for hitting you and resentful toward you at the same time for being so weak.

Regardless of the decisions you come to about your own position and future, do your best to keep your children in as sane an environment as you can. Never lie to them. Never tell them that all is well when it clearly isn't. If they see you beaten, hear you scream, and watch you weep, it is terribly confusing to them for you to say that nothing is wrong. If they are present during your husband's wild rampages and witness his destructive binges, it is inappropriate for you to tell them that their father is a wonderful man. Don't protect and make excuses for him.

On the other hand, children have a natural loyalty to their parents. This loyalty is evident even in children who are themselves abused. Do not deal with your anger toward your husband by constantly criticizing him before the children. This will wear them out, make them feel guilty about their affection for him, and cause them to resent you as a complainer. You need someone to whom you can pour out your troubles, but this person should be an adult. Do not expect your children to be your total support. They are only children. They need to be supported by you.

Neither total denunciation nor total denial is appropriate; the simple truth is best. Speak to your children about your situation. Help them deal with the realities of their father's behavior. Aim for a time when you are the least keyed up, the least fearful or angry, and can be the most dispassionate about your life. Allow them to ask questions about what is happening, and answer them as honestly as you can. Your children will perceive things differently from you. Listening carefully to their questions will give you an idea of their primary concerns and the areas where they need the most reassurance from you. Demonstrate your openness to questions—even painful ones—in the attitude you assume in answering them.

If you have decided separation is the best course to follow, explain to the children why and how this will help the family. One of your main concerns about separation may be the idea that your children need a father. You are right. Children do need both father and mother, but they need a good father and a good mother. Your husband's behavior is detrimental in many ways, even if he never attacks them physically. If you are in a violent marriage, your children *already* do not have a father. Counselor Lenore Walker says that children who have been living in violent homes experience tremendous relief when separated from their fathers. Doing without a father may be preferable to having a violent father. Separation offers at least a hope that your husband may get help, thus bringing closer the day the children may have the father they need.

Your separation will, no doubt, change your financial situation. Explain to the children that you will have to live more economically, and some of the "luxuries" might have to go. If you don't tell them, but hide the facts to spare them the worry, they won't understand what is happening and may feel they are being punished.

If you plan to stay with your husband no matter what, also give the children your reasons. Your plans affect them, too, after all. They deserve an explanation.

Do not condone your husband's violence. Your children are learning about adulthood from both of you. You do not want to give the impression that you approve of violent behavior. Your children *do* need good role models for adulthood. Since your home life is less than ideal for this purpose, try to find other adults to serve as surrogates. Encourage the children to spend time with friends whose parents have a healthy relationship and are open to taking an interest in your youngsters. Or, seek out neighbors, athletic coaches, teachers, fellow church members, relatives, scout troop leaders, anyone who is willing to take an active interest in helping a child grow up.

Keep an eye on your children's behavior. Watch for telltale signs of stress: frequent illness, poor grades or behavior problems in school, severe nervous habits, tendencies toward violence or withdrawal. Should such obvious indications of upset occur, getting professional help for them would be wise.

Above all, keep the lines of communication open between you and your young ones. Communication problems frequently coexist with domestic violence. Your children may be learning that violence is the way to solve problems. They need to learn to talk about their feelings rather than act them out. Watch them. Help them translate raw feelings into words. Show them that it is all right to be angry, afraid, or sad and to tell you when they feel those emotions. Start right now to do some preventive work on your children's behalf. You may save them from having a marriage like yours.

FROM A BATTERED CHRISTIAN WOMAN

"I can't think of anything that helped me more than coming to terms with my fear. Fear is the biggest obstacle a battered woman faces. I lived, ate, and slept in fear for thirty years. It robbed me of my strength. But when I gave over all my fear to the Lord, I felt as if a giant weight had been lifted from my shoulders.

"Pray for help to conquer your fear. It is your worst enemy—it paralyzes you. Once you lose it, you're not afraid to do anything you have to. Trust in

the Lord. He loves you so much. With His help you
can do what you must with courage and strength.''

> Fear not, for I have redeemed you;
> I have called you by your name;
> You are Mine.
> When you pass through the waters, I will be with
> you;
> And through the rivers, they shall not overflow you.
> When you walk through the fire, you shall not be
> burned,
> Nor shall the flame scorch you.
> For I am the LORD your God,
> The Holy One of Israel, your Savior (Isa.43:1–3).

8

How Can Her Friends Help Her?

But a certain Samaritan, as he journeyed, came where he was. And when he saw him, he had compassion on him, and went to him and bandaged his wounds, pouring on oil and wine; and he set him on his own animal, brought him to an inn, and took care of him. . . .Then Jesus said . . . "Go and do likewise" (Luke 10:33, 34, 37).

The case of the battered woman presents a challenge to those who wish to help her. She is a mass of conflicting emotions under the control of ever-present fear. She is unused to making decisions or taking the initiative in even the smallest matter. She sees her husband as omnipotent, and she fears taking help from others. She has learned that she is powerless to control her situation; convincing her otherwise is difficult. Yet she is a woman of many strengths, a survivor who has weathered countless storms and deserves admiration and respect as well as sympathy.

She may be your sister, your daughter, your niece. She may live next door, attend church with you, or serve on your committee at the PTA. She may be your client, your patient, your parishioner. What she needs is to be your friend, to feel you care about her.

Job, the biblical patriarch, poignantly expressed the need of the sufferer for the support of others when he said, "For the despairing man there should be kindness from his friend; Lest he forsake the fear of the Almighty" (Job 6:14 NASB).

Sometimes we have the tendency to avoid taking responsibility to help the suffering. We tell ourselves that the Lord has promised to look after them Himself. "Come to Me, all you who labor and are heavy laden, and I will give you rest" (Matt. 11:28).

But frequently in Scripture God used human helpers to accomplish the deliverance of His children from peril. Jochebed, Miriam, and Pharaoh's daughter saved the life of the infant Moses. A young Hebrew servant girl told Naaman how his leprosy could be healed. Jonathan helped

David to escape the clutches of King Saul. Ananias prayed for blind Paul in Damascus.

Jesus Himself best personified the spirit of mercy and concern for others that we are to have as Christians. He left us explicit instruction in His teachings. Of particular significance is His parable of the good Samaritan.

In this story Jesus told His followers, a man was robbed, beaten, and left for dead at the side of the road. Both a priest and a Levite, men of rank and prestige in the Jewish community, saw him lying there but walked away without stopping to help him. Then a Samaritan, traditional enemy of the Jews and scorned by them, not only risked his life by stopping to help the man—the robbers might still have been lurking nearby—but also paid out two days' wages to an innkeeper for the man's convalescence. He gave up his time and money and risked his life for this stranger. Could the message be any clearer?

It is a humiliating experience for a woman to admit she is abused and to ask for assistance.

"I think the one thing that helped me most was having a friend who matter-of-factly broached the subject with me and offered encouragement right away. 'Penny,' she said, 'you are a fine mother and a good person. I believe in you.' Knowing that I had that one solid support gave me the courage and determination to begin to work out a solution for myself."

A battered woman's friend can play a vital role in helping her cope with her circumstances. That friendship may even make the difference between life and death, but the task is not an easy one.

If you are the friend or relative of a battered woman, you may feel ambivalent about the situation. You may even be unsure of how appropriate it is for you to intervene in her life. Conflicts between mates are generally considered private family affairs that should be handled only by the parties involved.

"My husband says I should stay out of their life. He says I should be neutral."

Add to this uncertainty your affection for your friend and your frustration with her weakness and helplessness. You feel empathy and pity at the sight of her injuries and the sound of her weeping, and you cannot understand why she puts up with her husband. You feel exasperated that the problem goes on and on, that nothing is ever resolved with any degree of finality.

"How can she let herself get so badly injured and then go back for more? I wouldn't."

Your heart goes out to her, this miserable, suffering woman, and to her children who are forced to witness the daily violence, who appear so frail and vulnerable. Yet tucked away in a corner of your mind might be the smallest nagging thought that she does have some irritating character traits that could try the patience of any husband.

"Maybe she gets beaten because she is always whining at him and provoking him."

The whole situation is unsettling, and you find yourself annoyed with both husband and wife for creating such a state of affairs.

RECOGNIZE HOW SERIOUS THE SITUATION IS FOR HER

A crime is being committed repeatedly against this woman. She could be killed. Your friendship with her and your support may be the only things holding her together. You are an important part of her future recovery. Battered women, more than anything else, need people to believe in them, to take a chance and get involved in their lives.

"We battered women are basically a frightened, insecure group who need an outstretched hand."[1]

The abused woman needs someone who will not blame her or judge her, who will not remain uninvolved and indifferent. A friend who can tolerate her constant

177

apprehension and her need for encouragement, who does not panic with her but rather keeps an attitude of support, love, and confidence in her ability to cope, is a valuable ally.

As much as she needs encouragement and reassurance from you, your battered friend possibly needs patience more. She may never feel able to leave her battering relationship, and your acceptance of this possibility may be difficult. It will not be easy to understand and cope with her fear of making changes in her life. Leaving her husband will mean a significant loss for her, the loss of a longtime companion and the loss of her status as a "happily married" woman. She needs to be allowed time to make each decision about her future. She needs someone who can understand how hard it is for her to criticize her husband and come to grips with the fact that things won't get better on their own, someone who can encourage her to follow through *without pressuring her.*

Along with her other fears, she may well fear your disapproval of her indecisive behavior. After all, your support and involvement may be her most valuable asset. Don't judge her or criticize her for what you see as her weakness or her inability to take meaningful action. Don't harbor secret reservations about her situation. Don't wonder what she gets out of it or whether she enjoys it. Don't speculate about what she might do to provoke or upset her husband. No one deserves to be abused.

Be Prepared to Be Exhausted

Working with such a needy person is exhausting. Eventually the situation may take so much out of you that you "burn out." Frustrated with her paralysis and discouraged by the repetition of indignities and injuries she suffers without making a move to escape, you may be tempted to withdraw yourself and try to forget the whole thing. You may feel drained of emotional energy and disappointed that in spite of all her vows to the contrary, she repeatedly goes back to her old relationship unchanged. This burnout happens not only to friends and relatives of abused women but also to their counselors.

"It is hard to watch a drowning woman struggle, to invest yourself in trying to help her out of the water and then see her decide to try once more to swim by herself and pull away from your outstretched hand," says one domestic violence counselor.

Don't Let Her Become Too Dependent

On the other hand, you may do too much for her. You may want to step in and take over her life, planning what she will do, whom she will see, and where she will go. Don't do it. Don't let her transfer her total dependence on her husband to total dependence on you. It may feel good to both of you temporarily, but it reinforces her own sense of helplessness. You will end up being as much in control of her as her husband was. Remind yourself periodically that your friend has not only the right but also the responsibility to make her own decisions about her life and what she will do.

Don't Let Her Husband Influence You

Finally, beware of attempts on her husband's part to manipulate you into siding with him. Sarah was a battered woman who confided in her friend Jane about her plans to leave Barry. Tenderhearted Jane, saddened by the serious situation, offered to help in any way she could and eventually drove Sarah to a shelter for battered women while Barry was at work one day.

Barry was frantic when he found his wife gone. He attended prayer meeting the next night and openly confessed he might have "accidentally shoved Sarah a little in the heat of an argument," and she had run away from him in fear. "Now I just have to find her to apologize," he said.

Jane felt it her Christian duty to help bring the couple back together again. Having promised not to reveal Sarah's whereabouts, she nevertheless approached Barry with the idea of carrying messages back and forth between them. Barry was ecstatic.

Before long, Barry was phoning Jane once a day,

begging her to tell Sarah that he was sorry, that he had changed, and that he wanted another chance. Jane was taken in by his contrite behavior. She had not witnessed it for eight years and come to mistrust it as Sarah had. She could not understand Sarah's apparent hardheartedness in refusing to give Barry another chance.

Convinced that she had to do something to help, she went to the pastor of Barry and Sarah's church with the story and soon the two of them were calling and visiting Sarah, urging her to take Barry back once more. Sarah finally gave in to the pressure. Jane and the pastor were thrilled. They had saved a marriage.

Within four months of her return home, Sarah was hospitalized because of a miscarriage. Barry had beaten her severely, punching her repeatedly in the abdomen until the child was aborted.

Do not be taken in when an abuser proclaims his self-remorse or avows a change in his behavior. Do not let yourself be manipulated into taking his side or helping him compel his wife to return. Reuniting a couple temporarily may make you feel successful, but it could prove fatal to the abused wife.

If you find yourself caught in this position—between abuser and victim—tell him you are sorry that this is happening and urge him to get some counseling. But adamantly refuse to be his messenger.

To Help Realistically. . . .

1. Be available to talk whenever she needs it.

2. Listen sensitively to her. Take her problem seriously. Let her recount her horror stories to you.

3. Tolerate her expressions of anger. It is appropriate and healthy for her to be angry. She needs an outlet for this emotion that she has kept bottled up inside for so long. Encourage her to deal with her mixed up feelings *before* making any long-term plans. She will think more clearly and act more rationally after she has calmed down.

4. Build up her self-esteem. Remind her of her strengths and assets. Tell her how valuable she is. Show her you believe she can change her life. This should be among your top priorities.

5. Watch for printed material on domestic violence and share it. Find out about the problem so you understand her better. Pass on any literature—perhaps offering to keep it at your home if there is danger of her husband's discovering it.

6. Be her sounding board. Discuss her options. Help her identify her resources.

7. Assist her in setting reasonable goals, goals that are specific, realistic, action-oriented, and attainable. Even seemingly insignificant steps forward should not be taken lightly. If she works up the courage to insist on attending church, for example, it might seem quite a minor success, but it is a giant accomplishment for a woman who has never before insisted on anything. Keep in mind, however, that any step of self-assertiveness could prove fatal. Her husband will be very angry about her new independence. No action should be undertaken without prior consideration of the risks.

8. Be ready to discuss troublesome issues of her faith. Suggest a one-on-one Bible study dealing with her spiritual concerns. Never use Scripture to further oppress her or to put God on the side of a cruel and violent mate.

9. Act as a chauffeur when she needs transportation.

10. Help her locate a good counselor and a temporary shelter.

11. Hide her during a crisis.

12. Lend her money to get away or buy food and other necessities for herself and her children.

13. Store important items for her at your home—her extra money, clothes, baby goods, legal papers.

14. Take a special interest in her children. Look after them in emergencies. Invite them over to your house and get to know them. Show them by your own marriage how different life can be from what they see at home. Battered women have little energy to nurture their children. Some are even guilty of abusing their little ones. If you see that your friend is really having trouble handling the frustrations of motherhood, suggest a day-care center, for the children's sake and for hers.

15. Stand by your friend when she is discouraged by red tape, disbelief, skepticism, or the slowness of social service processes.

16. Help her do what SHE wants to do. You can make things better, but you can also make things worse. Don't urge her to do something she is not ready to do. She will only feel more inadequate and unhappy if she cannot bring herself to carry out your wishes.

17. If she makes the decision to leave her husband, be her friend and support during the days and weeks when she is trying to cope with the loneliness, the doubts, and the responsibilities of single parenthood.

18. If you are present when her husband attacks her, or if she runs to your home with her husband in hot pursuit, beware of trying to reason with him in that state. At that point, he is unreachable and could easily turn on you. The most helpful thing you can do is to provide your friend a means of escape—hide her in your home, for example. Offer to call police and serve as a witness when they arrive. If you do feel compelled to intervene physically between them—to save her life, perhaps—warn the husband in no uncertain terms that if he harms you, you will definitely press charges against him.

19. On a day-to-day basis, treat your friend's husband with cordiality and civility. You may feel awkward around him and be tempted to ignore him or even show your dislike for him. You may want to have a talk with him, criticizing the way he treats his wife and warning him to leave her alone. This could be disastrous for your friend. Remember that abusive husbands are jealous and possessive and try to isolate their wives. Don't antagonize him. If he senses your hostility, he will forbid his wife to see you.

Usually you have no need to fear for your safety when you are in the company of this man. He is generally a person who is only violent toward his wife. In fact, some abusive husbands are quite charming and socially outgoing on a superficial level. Beth's husband, George, was everybody's happy-go-lucky pal. If someone with such a mate confides to you that she is being mistreated, don't be skeptical just because her husband seems so nice. It is common for abusive men to appear gallant and congenial to outsiders.

Your friend has been the victim not only of her husband's abuse but also of countless rejections and disappointments from others. Your empathy can help make amends for their thoughtlessness and may be all she needs to begin to rebuild her life.

"How blessed is he who considers the help-less, The LORD will deliver him in a day of trouble" (Ps. 41:1 NASB).

HOW DOES THE CHURCH HANDLE CASES OF WIFE ABUSE?

The Christian faith boasts a long history of helping the needy. We can look back to our roots in Judaism and point, for example, to God's provision of cities of refuge for those in flight. Jewish laws provided for the feeding of the poor and hungry (see Lev. 19:9–10), the fair treatment of Gentiles (see Lev. 19:33–34), and the welfare of poverty-stricken Hebrews (see Lev. 25:25).

Since caring for the oppressed is a church tradition, we cannot neglect to extend a hand to the victims of domestic violence. Our track record on this issue is not impressive. The church's silence in the matter of family violence has not gone unnoticed by the secular world. In the eyes of some, that silence is seen as negligence that actually serves to perpetuate the problem.

It is also said that the church preaches male domi-nance, which battered wives and battering husbands perceive as condoning or even supporting abuse. The permanence and sanctity of the marriage bond are misused to forbid injured women to flee when their lives are threatened.

A director of one agency reports, "We received a call at the Center [for the Prevention of Sexual and

Domestic Violence] from a local shelter for abused women. The shelter worker indicated that she had a badly beaten woman there whose minister had told her to go back to her husband."[2]

"Victims are generally reluctant to contact their spiritual leaders. They're worried about how they'll be received,"[3] says another shelter director.

Churches can do much to rectify this matter. Their potential for making a significant contribution is great for several reasons.

First, churches are already places where people in trouble feel they can come for help. Clergymen deal with family and marital problems frequently.

Second, conservative Christians, who could never be reached by the secular press or feminist literature on abuse, can be touched and convinced by statements from the pulpit. They are skeptical of the world, but they trust their pastor.

Third, churches are teaching institutions, touching millions of lives with important material for everyday living. What churches teach about marriage, family relationships, and the biblical style of leadership can help to change attitudes and conditions that foster family violence.

Fourth, churches have authority. A pastor, the individual looked on as God's representative, speaks, as it were, with the voice of God. But this authority carries with it an awesome responsibility. If a clergyman tells a battered woman that what is happening to her is her fault, if he tells her she must suffer—to the death, if necessary—she may believe that God has spoken these words to her. Such advice could have calamitous results. Scripture warns us that those in authority in the church are accountable for what they teach: "My brethren, let not many of you become teachers, knowing that we shall receive a stricter judgment" (James 3:1).

Remember Job's friends who ostensibly came to console but actually spent their time condemning him instead? Their heartless comments intensified his suffering until it was nearly unendurable. Eliphaz said, "Who ever perished being innocent? Or where were the upright ever cut off?'' (Job 4:7). Bildad added, ''Behold, God will not cast away the blameless, nor will He uphold the evildoers'' (Job 8:20). Zophar reminded Job, ''Know therefore that God exacts from you less than your iniquity deserves'' (Job 11:6).

All of them spoke truth. They justified God's decision to allow Job to suffer. They defended His reputation and His right to govern the world as He wished. They were all on God's side, but in this context what they said misrepresented God. God said to them, ''My wrath is aroused against you and your two friends, for you have not spoken of Me what is right, as My servant Job has'' (Job 42:7).

Theologian J. Sidlow Baxter points out that God became angry with Job's friends because they nearly wrecked Job's soul more than even the Devil himself. He writes, ''Satan has no more dangerous tools than those who, under the guise of piety, and in the name of religious orthodoxy, offer false comfort or give untrue impressions of God.''[4]

Christians must guard against misrepresenting God to those who come to them for help. Although Job's friends praised God for His righteousness in all things, God admonished them for speaking wrongly of Him. They had neglected to comfort Job with the Lord's compassion and mercy.

Churches have not only the potential to help but also the moral obligation to do so. Some families in their pews are being torn apart by violence, violence that destroys them and alienates their children from Christian values. If churches want to save these families, they must waste no time in intervening when there is evidence of abuse.

Church involvement is crucial for battered wives with conservative religious backgrounds who may question how their faith relates to abuse. A pastor is the one authority who can help these women clear up spiritual misunderstandings that prolong their suffering unnecessarily. They may not be able to take spiritual comfort from secular counselors, but they may be willing to believe what their pastor says. Spiritual concerns are primary to many women, and their recovery will be significantly hampered without this pastoral encouragement.

HOW CHURCHES CAN HELP THE ABUSED WIFE

A church should be a place where all may come and know they will be protected, a place where violence is never taught or tolerated. A church should be a group of people who, by their actions, show that they are *for* the battered woman; they must not be neutral. In the case of domestic violence, being neutral is placing oneself on the side of the bully.

A church should offer shelter to victims of abuse. A shelter gives protection to the victim and also serves as a deterrent to an abusive husband. It provides him with solid evidence of the church's disapproval of his behavior, and it reminds him that his wife has a place to which she can flee if he continues his assaults.

It is a complicated and expensive task to set up and maintain a shelter for battered women—an undertaking many churches could not organize or finance. But other ways of sheltering battered women are within the means of a local congregation.

- Church members can offer their homes as emergency overnight shelters for desperate women who call.
- Funds can be set aside to put a woman and her children into a motel room until suitable alternative arrangements can be made, or to provide them with food and other necessities.
- The pastor, elders, or lay members of the congregation can offer themselves as advocates for the frightened women who otherwise feel so alone facing the police, the courts, and social service agencies.
- Volunteers from the congregation can be on call to give support and encouragement to women

sufficiently injured to require hospital emergency room care.

- Church members who have contact with the husband of a battered woman can urge him to get professional counseling, resisting the temptation to help him win his wife back until he does so.

HOW THE PASTOR CAN HELP THE ABUSED WIFE

As the shepherd of your congregation, you have the opportunity to help mold the thinking and the behavior of many people. You can do inestimable good and perhaps prevent numbers of cases of abuse by what you preach and teach from the pulpit.

Educate your parishioners about the marriage relationship in ways that do not victimize women. Explain that the biblical model of leadership, with Christ as the supreme example, is one of servanthood, not domination and heavy-handedness. Teach husbands to be the heads of their families as Christ is the head of the church—loving, nurturing, self-sacrificing.

Don't believe that your congregation is immune to this problem. Don't be indifferent. Keep current with the literature on abuse so that you can appreciate the battered woman's situation, her fears, and her concerns.

When couples with marital conflicts come to you for counseling, be alert for signs of abusive behavior. Speak with each mate *separately* at least once, and ask, "How do you fight?" Press for specific answers. If necessary, put it bluntly. "Do you ever hit your wife when you fight?" or "Are you ever hit by your husband when you fight?" The private conversation with each partner is essential. A wife will probably be unable to bring up the topic of abuse with her husband sitting beside her. This is a very important beginning for counseling couples in battering relationships.

Traditional couple counseling focuses on the causes of conflicts rather than how these conflicts are expressed. It is a common mistake for counselors to ignore the indications of abuse in their clients, assuming that once the underlying issues are cleared up, the physical violence will disappear on its own. It doesn't work that way.

No other issues can be dealt with while the wife is living in a state of intimidation. She is frozen in fear and cannot be expected to work on her relationship with her husband while he is still free to harm her. The husband, for his part, is unmotivated to make changes as long as he knows he can use brute strength to get his own way.

"We were in counseling for four years. Nothing ever changed. In fact, I received my worst beatings after each counseling session. I was afraid to bring this up during the sessions, and our counselor never once questioned my battered physical appearance."

Sensitive counseling is absolutely essential if you are going to be of help to a battered woman. Show her that you believe her, that she is not bad, that she need not feel guilty about what is happening to her.

This woman does not need to be told to be submissive. She has already been beaten into a state of total subjection. She places the blame for her situation on herself. If you confirm her guilt by implying that her condition is her fault, you destroy whatever small shreds of self-worth she may still possess.

The hope for true reconciliation lies in getting the wife to leave her husband, at least temporarily, to demonstrate that she will no longer endure abuse. You must help her to overcome her reticence to separate because of her faith. Without your help she may suffer extreme guilt when she goes to a shelter. She needs to be encouraged to see the separation in a positive light.

Never counsel a battered woman to stay with her husband "no matter what." At best your action may send her to seek help from a secular counselor who strongly advocates immediate divorce. At worst your counsel may be tantamount to signing her death warrant.

Instead, use your knowledge of Scripture and your authority as a church leader to comfort her. It is important that victims of violence not be offered mere slogans or flip advice by their pastors, such as "Trust in God," or "God will work things out." These unhelpful generalities only serve to make her feel she is not being taken seriously, and her suffering and pain are being disregarded. She must hear the tender voice of Christ speaking to her through you— therein lies real comfort. But commiserating with her is not enough. Jesus' words must be accompanied by significant concrete action on your part: shelter, money, transportation, food, clothing, day care for her children, advocacy with legal and social service systems, or referral to others who can help.

"I do not tell an abused woman from my congregation who comes to me for help to leave her husband. But I do say to her, as clearly and as pointedly as I can, that no one in the church and nothing in Scripture commands her to stay with a man who puts her life in jeopardy," says Pastor Daniel Keller. "I tell her that when a battering situation arises she should *firmly confront* her husband and that she should contact the Christian shelter in our city." He continues, "No pastor can be an expert in every social issue which confronts members of his congregation. He can, however, be enough aware of these issues to be able to refer his parishioners to appropriate sources of help."

If you feel uncomfortable attempting to handle such a case on your own, don't do it. Refer your parishioner to a community agency specializing in domestic violence. Keep in touch with the woman—and her husband, too, if possible. There will be time, when she is emotionally stabilized and has set some goals, for you to step back in and to help her with spiritual concerns she may still have. **Your work in PREVENTING abuse may be your biggest contribution to helping erase the problem.** Don't neglect the teaching aspect of any premarital counseling you do. Check out each prospective couple's communication skills. Emphasize the importance of talking things over together. Help the two partners to set up an equitable system for dealing with conflicts.

Over two hundred years ago Edmund Burke said all that was needed for evil to triumph was for enough good men to be silent. Don't let Satan continue to destroy families because you keep silent. Whether you are a relative of a battered woman, a friend, a neighbor, a pastor, or a counselor, you can make a difference in her life. Remember, the confirmation from heaven that this is indeed to be your work comes from the lips of Jesus. He said, "Assuredly, I say to you, inasmuch as you did it to one of the least of these My brethren, you did it to Me" (Matt. 25:40).

9

Is Reconciliation—
Not Just Patching It Up—
Possible?

In the middle of a large midwestern city, a faded red brick Victorian house three stories high stands in the shade of a single large sycamore tree. The trunk of the tree is scarred with countless carved initials, some hearts, and a few daggers. The house is awkwardly joined to a somewhat newer cement block structure that houses the Christian social service agency responsible for it.

Inside on the first floor, a lounge furnished in institutional vinyl and cast-offs provides communal space for the residents. There is a dining room adjacent, its tables squeezed close together to accommodate all the women. High chairs in various stages of disrepair line the wall next to the pass-through from the kitchen. The two upper floors of the house contain bedrooms, each with enough beds and cots for a woman and her children. There is no play space outside, but the basement has been converted to a playroom decorated with bright paintings of Fred Flintstone and his clan. Its floor is littered with toys.

People are everywhere. Women pace and worry, watch at the windows for angry husbands, keep counseling appointments next door, weep on one another's shoulders. Short-tempered mothers chase and scold mischievous youngsters who tease and pinch, slam doors, whine for snacks, and attempt to flush toys down the toilets. The ceaseless activity produces a buzz reminiscent of an agitated beehive but much less organized.

Nicknamed "the Lodge," it isn't a place you would ordinarily choose to be. Yet it is full. It is crowded to overflowing, in fact, and women have to be turned away for lack of room. What is its attraction? It is a place of safety. It is a shelter for battered women.

Shelters for victims of abuse are springing up in most major cities and quite a few smaller ones. While varied in appearance, they offer women similar services. The woman and her children are protected from further beatings and threats to their lives. They have an opportunity to recuperate from their wounds—physical and emotional—and to obtain legal and financial advice from concerned counselors. They also begin to redevelop some confidence in themselves and in their ability to make their lives better.

The women's movement is to be commended for its outcry against the mistreatment of women by the men they live with. That outcry first prompted the idea of sheltering the victims. Evangelicals, however, see a flaw in the feminist ideology because it may not contain any deep commitment to marriage as an institution worth preserving.

The counselors employed by some agencies seek to rescue the woman but have no concern for her marriage. To them, marriage may be a relationship no more or less important than any other. Therefore these counselors have little reason to try to salvage a union that is in such terrible trouble. They are also justifiably skeptical of the abuser's chances of reforming.

"Relationships that have been maintained by the man having power over the woman are stubbornly resistant to an equal power-sharing arrangement. . . . The best hope for such couples is to terminate the relationship," explains one counselor.[1]

When under the direction of counselors who do not concern themselves with saving marriages, a shelter may become primarily concerned with helping the victim rid herself of her husband as quickly and painlessly as possible as well as teaching her how to live independently.

On the surface, divorce *does* seem to be the only answer to the problem of domestic violence. It is extremely difficult for men who have been abusive with their wives to learn new responses to stress. Even Christians are drawn to the conclusion that a wife has only two choices—to stay and suffer the abuse or to divorce her mate. Beth's pastor saw only those two alternatives for her, and when he rejected divorce because of his faith, he was left with no other suggestion than for her to go home and try harder to work things out.

Can a Shelter Help Promote Reconciliation?

There is an alternative—the very thing that makes the Lodge different from many other shelters—the possibility of reconciliation between the married pair. The Lodge extends a hope to its clients that they may be denied elsewhere, the hope of restoring their marriages to what they should be. In addition to the counseling program for the women, there is a program for their husbands, and a series of joint counseling sessions for both.

WHAT IS THE BIBLICAL BASIS FOR RECONCILIATION?

Reconciliation is a basic tenet of the Christian faith. Through Christ's death and resurrection we are reconciled to God.

> Now all things are of God, who has reconciled us to Himself through Jesus Christ, and has given us the ministry of reconciliation, that is, that God was in Christ reconciling the world to Himself, not imputing their trespasses to them, and has committed to us the word of reconciliation (2 Cor. 5:18–19).

As we live our lives with Christ as our example we are admonished to reconcile ourselves to one another.

> Therefore if you bring your gift to the altar, and there remember that your brother has something against you, leave your gift there before the altar, and go your way. First be reconciled to your brother, and then come and offer your gift (Matt. 5:23–24).

Reconciliation involves replacing strain and hatred with peace and fellowship. Between the partners in an abusive marriage, reconciliation is extremely difficult. The conflict runs deep and is usually longstanding. But the potential for healing the marriage is there, if both partners can face the destructive nature of their relationship and commit themselves to change it. Getting this commitment from a violent husband is difficult but not impossible.

Many professionals who work with abused women take a dim view of the word *reconciliation*. To them reconciliation means sending the woman back to her husband and patching things up between them with a kiss-and-make-up and try-once-more attitude. At the Lodge reconciliation means something entirely different.

"We see ourselves as peacemakers," explains the director of the agency and administrator of the Lodge. "But by peacemaker we do not in any way mean to imply that we simply push the couple back together. Before husband and wife can live together in peace, the marriage must change substantially. As peacemakers we attempt to create harmony out of discord. We do not ignore or minimize the conflict. We do not apply 'Band-Aids' over the tears. Rather we work together with the two individuals to build up their own strengths, and then we slowly and painstakingly work at reweaving the fabric of the marriage."

Counselors in secular agencies agree with this approach.

"What we have to do in psychotherapy," comments one, "is teach each one [of the couple] to be independent people, then they may be able to make an interdependent relationship. Until each one of them feels whole and able to stand on his and her own, they will not be able to do it."[2]

How to Be Admitted to the Lodge

The Lodge, like other shelters, offers first of all a place of safety. Women in crisis come at all hours of the day and night.

"It is inadvisable to take lightly the danger that these women say they are in," one of the coordinators explains. "Over the past few years, domestic conflicts have resulted in the deaths of ten of our clients. We keep the doors locked at all times, and we suggest to the women that they not divulge their location to anyone."

"It is a tremendous shock for the men when their wives leave to get help," adds another counselor, who works directly with the husbands. "They will do just about anything to get them back. We have had children snatched out of our waiting room next door. We have had to contend with men who nearly camp out on our doorstep, just waiting for their wives to set foot outside, and men who call on the phone and harass us at every hour of the day and night for weeks at a time."

Not all admissions to the Lodge are dramatic. A few couples come in together after recognizing that their relationship is in serious trouble. At other times, a husband who has been arrested for assaulting his wife is referred to the Lodge by the court for mandatory counseling as an alternative to a jail sentence. In that case, his wife may or may not choose to take part in the women's program.

Some clients arrive fairly calmly, having made their "escape plans" at an earlier time. For others, like Marianne, immediate shelter is a matter of life and death, and they arrive with husbands in hot pursuit. The day that Marianne came to the Lodge, she had barely slipped through the door before her husband appeared, brandishing a knife and screaming threats through the door. Inside, bruised and sore, she huddled in a corner while staff members reassured her of her safety.

A staff member went out to face the irate husband. "He was completely unapproachable. We tried to calm him down, but he had that knife and was absolutely determined to drag his wife home with him. In the end, we had to call the police."

Sometimes women do not quite reach the door. In Ellie's case, the Lodge staff heard screaming outside the building and went to investigate. They saw her on the doorstep, clutching her four-year-old daughter while her husband tried to wrench the child from her grasp. Only the wailing siren of an approaching police car frightened him away, and mother and child were able to be brought safely inside.

"It is amazing to see the sudden new levels of energy and emotional stability in the women when they finally realize they are safe," one counselor commented. "These are incredibly strong women, not the stereotyped, bedraggled weaklings that some might think. They have lived for years under tremendous strain and have coped repeatedly with the threat of imminent death. Most of their energy has been centered on staying alive, protecting their children, and living out the lie that all is well. There has been little left over for anything else such as personal growth, decision making, and so on. But take away the terror, and many spring back with amazing speed to regain self-confidence, learn self-sufficiency, and begin taking charge of their lives."

For others, relearning these skills comes more slowly. One of the Lodge policies is that any woman may be admitted as many times as she needs to be. Many women have second thoughts soon after they arrive. Home ties are strong and contrite husbands quite convincing. It often takes several short separations to prove to some of the women that their husbands' promises are not trustworthy and that they need not feel guilty staying away until their mates get professional help.

"The first time we interview a battered woman we want her to tell us her story," says the supervisor. "It may be that we are the first ones who have ever believed her."

Some women have never confided in anyone who took their problems seriously. Beth's beatings were ignored by her physician and belittled by her pastor. Other women have been told outright that their husbands should be allowed to do as they please. Still others have found themselves the objects of contempt by family members and friends. Being given the chance to tell all to someone who can assure them their problem is real sometimes unleashes a virtual torrent of pent-up emotions.

"There is so much to say, so much to get off her chest, that this initial interview could last several hours. When it is over, the woman usually feels a whole lot better and the listening staff member is exhausted!" adds the supervisor.

When the battered woman is more informed about the subject of wife abuse, she will feel less alone in her dilemma. Many wives are incredulous when they hear the dynamics of the violent relationship described to them. "Why, that's my marriage exactly," they are apt to say. "I feel as if you are describing my husband and me." Great relief comes from the knowledge that others face the same problem. Those who grew up in violent homes and assume that all marriages follow this same pattern are encouraged when they discover that marriage need not be violent.

Once the terror of the crisis is past, the woman must face her ambivalent emotions. On the one hand, she loves her husband, and at times his behavior is very endearing—especially now that she is away from him and he is trying to win her back. On the other hand, she feels tremendous anger for all the grief, pain, and heartache he has caused her through the years. She vacillates between love and hate, anger and terror, wanting to go home and wanting to stay away. She possesses optimism and pessimism about her situation, feeling safe and feeling vulnerable simultaneously.

Much time must be spent sorting through these feelings in an effort to come to a place of forgiveness. Unless she can take this step she will never fully recover from her experience, and it is a very difficult step. She has heard her husband's innumerable insincere confessions and vows of repentance. She has repeatedly forgiven her mate only to find herself under attack once more. At some point she can no longer believe him, and frustration and anger hinder further attempts to forgive. Caring professional counselors point out that she can forgive but also confront her mate with the need for outside help in learning how to control himself.

The victim of abuse may feel in her confusion that forgiving her husband means allowing him to abuse her again. It is helpful to have support and reassurance from a Christian counselor while she works through these feelings to understand that her forgiveness does not mean the acceptance of abuse.

Group Sessions

One of the most vital aspects of the Lodge program is the support the women receive from one another in the evening discussion groups. Many of the women have been kept so isolated that this may be the first close contact they have had with other women for years. They hunger for camaraderie and friendship, offering one another sympathy, suggestions, tangible and intangible supports, even advice on the practical day-to-day aspects of their lives. They strengthen each other's fledgling self-confidence and understand one another in a way the staff members cannot.

Decision-making

Staff members offer the reconciliation alternative to all their clients but make a point of encouraging the women to make their own decisions. For each woman, all possible options are reviewed and discussed. Reconciliation is only an option for a woman whose husband is willing to cooperate. Without his participation, reconciliation is impossible. A number of women do not have this choice.

"We try to be as much help as possible," says the shelter's supervisor. "We give support to whatever move the woman feels is right for her. There are times when we feel we can see perfectly clearly what needs to be done. And in cases like that it is extremely tough to keep ourselves from stepping in and running the woman's life for her—especially when it is clear she wants us to! But part of our job is to help her regain the confidence to make her own decisions so we resist the temptation to push in one direction or the other. There are times when the temptation is almost overpowering.

"We had a client a year ago who had nearly died from a severe beating. When she told us about her husband we could not believe she had stayed with him as long as she had. While she was at the Lodge, he phoned frequently, threatening to kill, not only her, but us too, if she didn't come home. He was especially frightening because he had a family history of horrible violence.

"Janet vowed solemnly that she would never return to him unless he got help first. But he resisted. Over several months he gradually wore down her resolve with pleadings and threats and promises until one day she blurted out to me—somewhat embarrassed, I think—that she had decided to go back to him and give him another chance. Never before had I come so close to trying to persuade any woman *not* to go ahead with a decision she had made."

The message of the gospel is an important ingredient in counseling battered women, but the timing of the presentation of the message must coincide with their readiness to hear. Any battered woman at the Lodge is a jumble of contradictory emotions. She is concentrating on staying alive. She wonders if her bad marriage is all her fault. She worries about her children and their reaction to her move. She grapples with high levels of anger and bitterness toward her mate. If she is a Christian, she will also be experiencing guilt and shame over her separation— however temporary and justified.

When she first arrives at the Lodge and is dealing with all these issues at once, the staff allow her to take the lead in initiating a discussion of the spiritual dimensions of her situation. For some women it is a primary concern. In these cases, spiritual encouragement and examination of pertinent Bible passages immediately bring comfort and support.

Some, however, reject all references to religion, often because of an experience with an unsympathetic Christian. When that is the case, biblical discussions are left for a time when the woman is feeling more settled and emotionally stabilized. Insisting she come to terms with her faith at a time when she is not ready for it only compounds a battered woman's anxiety and confusion.

The nonbeliever in crisis may or may not be ready to deal with a new understanding of the place of Christ in her life when she already has so many dilemmas confronting her. On the other hand, the gospel message of love and deliverance, explained gently when she is feeling homeless and adrift, may give her the strength she needs to get through the worst days. Sensitive Christian counselors make judgments as individual cases arise. Needless to say, the same approach to spiritual matters will not work for everyone, and although this aspect of counseling is not neglected, it is not a magic key that immediately unlocks the door to emotional health and the good life for every battered woman.

A Christian supervisor at another center for victims of abuse says, "when people are angry, they rarely turn to God." She, too, believes in waiting with spiritual matters until the women have come to terms with their situation and have been able to make some decisions about their lives. She believes God is patient enough to be able to wait for these women to be ready to hear. "God can handle [the wait]," she says. "I just hope I can."[3]

WHAT DOES THE BIBLE SAY ABOUT SEPARATION?

If the Lodge considers reconciliation its ultimate goal, some may wonder, how can the staff encourage separation between mates? By taking this woman, they sanction her decision to leave her husband. A cardinal scriptural principle is broken here, for the Bible says, "Therefore what God has joined together, let not man separate" (Mark 10:9). The apostle Paul restates this in 1 Corinthians 7:10: "Now to the married I command, yet not I but the Lord: A wife is not to depart from her husband." How can Christians advocate separation of the marital partners and still maintain that they are faithful to Christ's teachings?

It is true that temporary separation is a vital aspect of the program at the Lodge, but it isn't the separation that breaks up the marriage. The violence has already done that. To say that separation breaks up abusing families is like blaming a dentist for a toothache. The separation is a step toward reconciliation. It is not the beginning of the death of the marriage, or an end in itself. It is necessary and integral to the eventual healing of the relationship.

"We certainly aren't advocating that the couple part for good," says the agency director. "Separation carries with it the connotation of breaking apart, but what we are ultimately after is a reunion."

Temporary separation is needed for several reasons. In the beginning the woman needs physical protection from her husband. The counselors at the Lodge cannot in good conscience send a woman back into an abusive situation knowing that the abuse will get worse. Since violence in battering relationships tends to escalate, many feel that it is only a matter of time before one of the partners kills the other.

Aside from that, a battered woman living with her husband must concentrate on pleasing him and keeping peace at home. She has no time or energy to spare for anything that does not relate to survival. It is unfair to expect her to take on the burden of working through deep-seated marital problems with this amount of stress already on her shoulders. A temporary separation gives her time and space to gather her strength. Then she *can* work with her mate toward a satisfactory relationship.

The abusive husband needs the separation as well, although no husband in this position would ever acknowledge that fact at the outset. *But separation is usually the only thing that will motivate him to change.* He is dominant and controlling, yes, but he is also incredibly dependent on the woman he mistreats. He cannot stand the thought of losing her. As long as she puts up with his behavior, he is happy with the status quo. When she leaves, his life tips into a state of crisis. He needs her desperately, and her departure can prompt him to seek help for himself in an effort to get her to come back to him. It is rare to find a husband who is truly motivated to change while his wife is still living with him.

Certainly the words of 1 Corinthians 7:10 cannot be ignored. But Paul goes on to add in verse 11, "But even if she does depart, let her remain unmarried or be reconciled to her husband." The Greek word translated *reconcile* in this verse means "to change mutually." And this is what temporary separation is designed to promote—mutual changes in the couple to restore their relationship.

How Does the Husband Feel about Separation?

When his wife leaves him, the abusive husband is thrown into tremendous turmoil. He feels hurt and betrayed that his wife would turn on him in this way. A typical response may sound something like this:

"Sure, I roughed her up a little. Looking back, I think I probably went too far. I just let myself go at the wrong moment. I was only trying to teach her a lesson. I just got a bit out of control. I never meant to hurt her like that.

"After I got hold of myself and looked at her, I felt pretty bad. Her face was kind of messed up—a little swollen and bruised—and I knew I couldn't let her go out of the house until she looked better. So I forbid her to go to the doctor or anything, and I locked her in.

"I took real good care of her. I fed her soup and egg nog. She couldn't eat solid food because her jaw wouldn't work right. I came home from work during the day to tend her, and I was the best nurse anyone could ever have wished for. I had compassion for her and took pity on her.

"And do you know, that lousy bitch betrayed me! As soon as she was well enough to get out of bed she broke out of the house and ran to the police.

How could she do that to me? How could she betray me to the cops—her own husband who loved her and fed her and looked after her injuries like I did? After all I did for her!

"Now here I am. I have to be in this counseling program or go to jail. I have a police record, I suppose, and only her to blame for it."

The work with abusive husbands at the Lodge is divided into three phases: first, stopping the abuse; second, developing awareness of emotions; and third, resocializing.

The first phase occurs on a one-on-one basis with Dan, the men's counselor.

"Because his only reason for being in the program is his belief that this will get him his wife back, a man usually comes to us pretty guarded and defensive. So we ask. 'What can you do to get your wife back?' We help him to see that stopping his abuse is the only thing that will make his wife come home. After the physical violence is under control we begin to work on attitudes. Over a period of time he must come to face the fact that battering his wife is inappropriate and that he does not have the *right* to do it."

Through counseling, the abusive husband is slowly, but relentlessly, brought to the place where he takes responsibility for his own actions. In the beginning if he hits his wife it is because *she* burned his toast or *she* made some remark he did not like. Eventually he admits that he hit her because *he* decided to hit her.

Abusive men must also learn they cannot hide behind the old notion of being out of control. "I got so mad I just didn't know what I was doing," they say. "It's not my fault." Direct confrontation forces them to see just how much control they do have over their actions. A typical counseling session may run something like this:

> *Counselor:* Please tell me about the last time you were violent with your wife.

205

Client: Oh, I've never been violent with her. We just fight a lot.

Counselor: Tell me about your last fight. What happened?

Client: She told me that my pants didn't coordinate with my shirt. She's always telling me I don't look right.

Counselor: What do you do in response?

Client: I told her they were fine. I can dress myself. But she wouldn't listen to me.

Counselor: What did you do when she wouldn't listen to you?

Client: She started walking away, so I just turned her around so she would listen to me.

Counselor: How did you turn her around?

Client: Oh, I don't remember. I just put my hand on her shoulder and turned her around.

Counselor: Demonstrate to me how you did that.

Client: Well, I did grip her shoulder a little bit, but she bruises so easily.

Counselor: Then what happened?

Client: She started screaming and hollering. I wasn't doing a thing.

Counselor: So then what did you do?

Client: I forget. Everything happened so fast. Maybe I slapped her a little on the face to calm her down.

Counselor: How did you slap her on the face?

Client:	*I just barely touched the side of her face.*
Counselor:	Was your hand open or closed?
Client:	*Open, of course! I'd never hit a woman with my fist!*
Counselor:	So you decided to slap her with your hand instead of your fist. If you were out of control, how come you didn't go ahead and kill her?
Client:	*I wouldn't kill anyone.*
Counselor:	Were you in a public place when this happened?
Client:	*No. This is just something between me and my wife.*
Counselor:	So you decided that you could hit her with your open hand, but not your fist. You decided to hurt her a little, but not kill her, and you decided to do it in private, because it was no one else's business. It seems to me you were doing a lot of thinking and making a lot of decisions for a man out of control.[4]

"These men have never handled their feelings any other way than by lashing out. To them it is a brand-new idea when I suggest that they go for a walk to cool down if they feel themselves getting edgy, or even simply leave the room. I've told them to go sit in their car with the windows rolled up and scream too," Dan says.

Since abusers tend to be lacking in self-control, they rely on others to set limits for them. Talking with an authority figure like Dan, or facing a judge who requires them to have counseling, can help them control their behavior.

If violence resumes at home anytime during the months of counseling, it is regarded as a very serious offense. The counseling is ended immediately, and the abusive man sees his chances of getting his wife back diminish before his very eyes. If he has been referred for counseling by the court, the criminal justice system is notified of his breach of conduct.

Before they move into the next phase and become part of a group, the men are also educated about domestic violence. It is stressed to them that violent behavior destroys any hope of a true loving partnership between them and their wives.

Men's Group Sessions

The rest of the treatment centers on the men's group sessions. These are evening meetings held in an informal setting with the men interacting around a specific topic of discussion. In the group men find themselves developing friendships and receiving support from others with similar problems.

Two counselors, Dan and Linda, lead the group, helping the men talk through their frustrations, encouraging them to offer help to one another, and keeping the focus of the discussion on the men and not their wives. It is a long, slow process, because these men must rethink so much about themselves and the way they live.

They tend to justify their behavior by attributing all sorts of evil motives to their wives.

"She is just waiting for the chance to run off with some guy. I have to keep her locked in the house while I'm at work."

"She only cares about the children. She doesn't ever have time for me. She deliberately spends time with them to make me jealous."

"Somebody went behind my back to have me removed from the church council, and I know it was her."

Much group time is spent in resocializing the men. Once they have their actions and emotions under control, their basically destructive underlying beliefs may be tackled. In general, they need to develop more respect for women. This aspect of the work is particularly slow.

"You can't trust skirts."

"Women are out to get you. They're only interested in your money."

"Leave a woman alone for one minute, and she'll be flirting with every man in sight."

Linda's presence in the group gives the men practice relating to women as equals. Although they tend to ignore her at first, she quietly but firmly commands their respect.

Group members redefine what maleness is and learn they can be sympathetic, kind, even frightened or unsure of themselves without endangering their masculinity. The abusive husband needs to develop self-esteem as much as his wife does. Up to this point, in order to maintain his fragile self-confidence, he has always had to be right, or at least to have the last word. Now he must learn to accept the fact that he may sometimes be wrong, without losing his sense of self-worth.

WHEN SHOULD THE UNBELIEVING HUSBAND HEAR THE GOSPEL?

Finally, if he is a nonbeliever, he needs to hear the message of true liberation in Christ. It may seem out of place for the spiritual emphasis to come last in the program. In fact, the counselors at the Lodge have been criticized more than once for this seeming reversal of priorities.

"What you need to do," onlookers have suggested, "is to get these men saved right away."

We know our God is a God of miracles. We have seen exciting supernatural changes in people who undergo conversions. Without question, conversion of an abusive husband could change his life and his relationship with his wife overnight. The Lodge counselors do not deny this.

The reason they do not discuss the gospel earlier in the program is that a man desperate to get his wife back will agree to anything he thinks might get her to come home to him. If a testimony of religious conversion will do the trick, he is willing to try it. Many of the wives have spent years praying for just that. Since there is no way of knowing immediately whether the conversion is real or simply a ploy to get him out of an uncomfortable situation, it is unwise to put this escape route in his hands.

"Of course we are anxious for these men to come to a saving knowledge of Christ. But we don't want to tempt them to confess a phony salvation in order to avoid really changing," Linda says.

For abusive Christian husbands who come for counseling, the spiritual issues are clarified immediately. It is essential that these men not be allowed to continue thinking their violent behavior is in any way scripturally based. True biblical leadership is discussed with them from the very beginning to give them a focus for their changes.

Joint Counseling Sessions

During months of counseling, husband and wife are seen separately because they have different issues to resolve in their lives. During this time each has his or her own counselor because both husband and wife need to be assured that they are getting the full attention they require. Also, neither spouse should be seen to be gaining the support of the counselor in the presence of the other.

The joint sessions begin when husband and wife have developed sufficient strength as individuals to begin to work on the relationship together. The first sessions are usually awkward because both husband and wife are a little afraid. The wife fears that the old pattern of control and intimidation will begin anew. The husband fears being rejected by this new woman, one he feels might have been turned against him during their months of living apart. Both may be anxious but hopeful, uncertain of the future and uncertain of themselves.

"She's changed. She used to be so warm and forgiving. She's different now. I don't think she'll want me anymore."

"I sometimes feel cold—like a rock—afraid to let myself go and love and trust him like I once did, for fear I'll be hurt again."

Gradually as the sessions continue, with the counselors present to help the flow of the discussions, control issues and other conflicts from the past can be dealt with.

First, of course, the dominating authority and tyrannical control the husband has wielded in the relationship must be removed. A place of respect and partnership must be created for the wife. Counselors at the Lodge sometimes suggest very practical strategies for altering the power imbalance that has characterized the relationship.

"It may be a matter of opening a joint checking account," Cathy explains, "or setting up a schedule where Mary gets one night out a week while John stays home with the children. Both of these ideas may sound elementary, but to these couples they represent quite revolutionary changes in thinking."

As the couple gradually eases back into a relationship, it looks to the outsider as if they are courting. Actually, in a sense, it is a courtship. John must prove himself to Mary all over again. She must learn to trust and love him.

The joint counseling sessions continue until violence is no longer an issue and until there is a balance of power in the relationship.

"Both husband and wife usually think these sessions will be easier than they are. They have been living apart, each more relaxed because the main source of his stress—his spouse—is absent. But when they come together again all the old feelings may recur. What used to bother the one about the other is still there," says one of the counselors.

The staff watch for specific behaviors that indicate to them that the husband and wife are making progress. The husband, for example, begins to allow his wife to have differences of opinion with him. When he can tolerate this without showing stress, he has come a long way in rebuilding himself. Similarly, when the wife can express herself openly and feel free to participate in activities outside the home that do not include her husband, she is showing her new personal strength.

The last phase of the reconciliation counseling centers on building better communication skills, helping the couple to set new marital goals, and teaching them healthy ways to resolve the disagreements arising between them as they continue their life together.

"We don't see many couples pursue this reconciliation to the very end," a counselor admits. "The faulty relationship patterns in abusive marriages are so deeply ingrained in the husband and wife that the road to rebuilding their life is very long and rocky indeed. Few couples have the patience, the determination, and the strength to see it through. But I think that it is very important that we offer this alternative because of the value we place on the permanence of the marriage bond. There is no doubt that God's desire is for married couples to stay married."

10
What Happened to Beth?

For another ten years I lived in perpetual dread, without hope of rescue or expectation of reprieve. Fear kept me there. I was paralyzed and incapable of planning any action that might improve the situation for George and me.

But one day I was listening to a talk show on the radio and heard a domestic violence counselor from a local shelter describe George and me perfectly.

"I'm a battered wife," I said aloud, understanding dawning at last. "A battered wife." I touched the bandage that covered my ear and thought, *I can go talk to them. They know what I'm going through.*

At the shelter a soft-spoken young woman counselor heard me out and assured me that my story was not unusual or shameful. We talked for several hours.

"How can I end this?" I finally asked her. "How can I get through to George?"

We went over all the options. "Probably at some point you'll have to leave again," she told me. "Until you do, George will not have any incentive to change."

I knew she was right. I knew I had to get out, but I just couldn't take that first step. George's warning of reprisal was there in front of me all the time.

Then one day she put this question to me. "Beth, what is the worst thing George could do to you if you leave?"

Without a bit of hesitation I answered, "Why, kill me, of course."

"And which would be worse for you, to be killed or to go on living the way you are right now?"

It was as if a light suddenly went on. How simple! "I'd rather be dead," I answered.

She nodded. "George is never going to get better until you show him that you will not accept his behavior. As long as you continue to put up with it, you are telling him that what he does to you and the children is okay."

Those words rang in my ears. George needed help, and I was standing in his way. I had to leave him until he went for help. I walked home, my decision firmly made.

The next day I was admitted to the shelter.

Right now George and I are living apart. I have explained to him that I cannot return until he gets counseling. So far he is resisting.

I'm not going to divorce George. I don't know what the Lord wants for us, but I know He doesn't want me to divorce. If George should come to me and say that he has found someone else he wants to marry, then I wouldn't stand in his way. If he seeks to be released, I won't put up a fight. However, I still look forward to the day the Lord will work in George's life, and we will be able to pick up the pieces and be the couple God wants us to be. I want that very much.

I've come through the fear, and I'm living in hope. I don't know how this will all work out, but I know that I have finally put George where he belongs—in the Lord's hands.

Addendum: The Battered Husband

The pervasive view of domestic violence is that it is a crime perpetrated by men against women. The idea of women battering their partners conjures up images of old Andy Capp cartoons depicting Andy's wife in bathrobe and curlers, waiting for him at the door, foot tapping impatiently, rolling pin in hand, ready to let him have it. To most, it's a joke.

Yet, violent women do exist. Each year shelter workers find they answer phone calls from a few male victims. Police reports indicate that they, too, encounter abusive women occasionally on domestic disturbance calls. And there are bound to be those cases that never come to light because the men are too embarrassed or "noble" to come forward with complaints.

In drawing conclusions on violent women from raw research data, it is important to keep the woman's motive for violence in mind. Some women become violent protecting themselves from abuse. When being assaulted, the law says, a woman is justified in using enough force to stop the attack. Some women are violent in situations where both partners are angry and engaging in mutual combat. Neither of these cases constitutes husband abuse. True abuse occurs when the woman is the sole violent partner and uses tyrannical behavior to dominate and coerce her mate.

Some studies show that, except in cases where the wife is being abused, very few women are violent. Other studies show that the rates of wife-to-husband and husband-to-wife violence are equal. To say that equal numbers of men and women are violent doesn't tell the whole story, however. It is necessary to recognize that because of a woman's smaller size and weight, a hit by a man and a hit by a woman do not have equal potential for injury.

This is not to say that legitimate cases of husband

abuse are non-existent. In a culture such as ours, where children are exposed to large amounts of approved violence (TV, movies, videos), it would be surprising if there were *not* women who resorted to physical aggression with their mates.

Though the research in this area is very limited, women who are abusive seem to demonstrate many of the characteristics of violent men. They believe that their partner must be made to act more appropriately, that control of the relationship is their right and that violence and nonphysically abusive tactics are the best means to obtain that control. Moreover, they use their smaller size and the laws of chivalry to defend their prerogative to hit but not be hit back. They often come from violent families where they witnessed or experienced abuse as children. They have grown up with low self-esteem, feelings of inadequacy and insecurity, emotional dependency needs, and poor relationship skills. They frequently find it difficult to communicate effectively and harbor great reserves of anger. Add stressors that build tension, such as financial worries, alcohol or drug abuse, sexual frustrations, job insecurity, and the constant demands of their children, and the stage is set for violence.

Violent women and their spouses need the same help as violent men and theirs. Abused husbands must be regarded as legitimate victims of crime and treated with respect. They deserve the same support and protection that battered women have come to receive. As husband abuse comes more to public awareness, counselors and helping agencies such as shelters and churches will have to broaden their treatment agendas to include this facet of family violence.

Notes

Chapter 2

1. Joan O'Connor, "Coalition To Launch Campaign Against Domestic Violence," *Psychiatric News* (July 3, 1987).

2. *Uniform Crime Reports 1986,* Federal Bureau of Investigation, JUS–432 (release date, July 25, 1987).

3. O'Connor, *Psychiatric News.*

4. Murray Straus, "Wife Beating: How Common and Why?", *Victimology: An International Journal,* vol. 2, no. 3–4 (1977–78): 443–58.

5. *Plain Talk about Wife Abuse,* National Institute of Mental Health (July 29, 1987).

6. Lenore Walker, *The Battered Woman* (New York: Harper Colophon, 1979), 19.

7. Bill Peterson, "System Frustrates Battered Wives," *Washington Post,* 2 Nov. 1974.

8. Wesley Monfalcone, *Coping With Abuse in the Family* (Philadelphia: Westminster, 1980), 18.

9. "Editor's Note," *Family Life Today* (April 1983): 5.

10. "Center Sponsors Class for Abused Women," *Working Together* (Nov.–Dec. 1983): 5.

11. Howard Green and Cathy Suttor, "A Christian Response to Domestic Violence: Reconciliation Model for Social Workers," (Indianapolis: Salvation Army Family Service Department, 1983), 4.

12. Walker, *The Battered Woman,* 55.

13. *Indianapolis News,* 21 Aug. 1981.

14. *Indianapolis News,* 7 Feb. 1981.

15. *Greenville (Indiana) News,* 13 May 1981.

16. *Peoria (Illinois) Journal-Star,* 19 July 1981.

17. *Charade,* Universal Studios, 1964.

18. Sherman Edwards and Hal David, "Johnny Get Angry," (New York: Tod Music Inc., 1962).

19. Betsy Light, "Today's Screen Heroines Dehumanized, Abused," *Indianapolis Star,* 19 Sept. 1983.

20. Betsy Light, "Teen Sex Films: Funny or Foul?" *Indianapolis Star,* 18 Sept. 1983.

21. "Premarital Violence: Battering on College Campuses," *Response* (July–Aug. 1981): 1.

22. Harold LeDoux, "Judge Parker," *The Camden (New Jersey) Courier Post,* 1 Jan. 1984.

23. Terry Davidson, *Conjugal Crime* (New York: Hawthorne, 1978), 112.

24. Terry Davidson, "Wife Beating: A Recurring Phenomenon Throughout History," *Battered Women,* ed., Maria Roy (New York: Van Nostrand Reinhold, 1977), 11.

25. Elizabeth Gould David, *The First Sex* (New York: Putnam, 1971), 255.

26. William Mandel, *Soviet Women* (Garden City: Anchor Books, 1975), 13.

27. Roger Langley and Richard C. Levy, *Wife Beating: The Silent Crisis* (New York: E. P. Dutton, 1977), 39.

28. Ginny McCarthy, *Getting Free* (Seattle: The Seal Press, 1982), 4.

29. "New Sentence Draws New Fire," *Indianapolis News,* 30 June 1983.

Chapter 3

1. Military families seem particularly prone to abuse. Often subsisting at poverty level, these young couples are subjected to separation from each other, isolation from their extended families, and frequent moves from base to base. Overseas, a military wife is often completely dependent on her husband and feels the weight of her second-class status even in her military designation "dependent." Isolation and dependency, coupled with the realization that reporting abuse could jeopardize her husband's career, keep her trapped in the abusive situation.

2. Suzanne K. Steinmetz, *The Cycle of Violence* (New York: Praeger, 1977), 118.

3. Sandra McDade, "Don't Let Battering Destroy the Family," *USA Today,* 12 Dec. 1983.

4. Anne L. Ganley, *Court-Mandated Counseling for Men Who Batter* (Washington, D.C.: Center For Women Policy Studies, 1981), 34.

5. Richard Gelles, *The Violent Home* (Beverly Hills: Sage Publications, 1972), 117.

6. Mary Claire Blakeman, "His Cocaine High Can Be a Traumatic, Devastating Experience for Her," *The Camden (New Jersey) Courier Post*, 7 Sept. 1983.

7. Mildred Daley Pagelow, "Preliminary Report on Battered Women" (Paper presented at the Second International Symposium on Victimology, Boston, Mass., Sept. 5–11, 1976): 15.

8. O'Connor, *Psychiatric News*.

9. Walker, *The Battered Woman*, 43.

10. "Dear Abby," *Indianapolis News*, 9 June 1983.

11. Gelles, *Violent Home*, 171.

12. Walker, *The Battered Woman*, 146.

13. Gelles, *Violent Home*, 173–74.

Chapter 4

1. *Gesenius's Hebrew-Chaldee Lexicon to the Old Testament* (Grand Rapids: Baker, 1979), 619.

2. Letha Scanzoni and Nancy Hardesty, *All We're Meant to Be* (Waco: Word, 1974), 27.

3. H. C. Leupold, *Exposition of Genesis* (Grand Rapids: Baker, 1942), 137.

4. Grantly Dick-Read, *Childbirth Without Fear* (New York: Harper and Brothers, 1959), 43.

5. Russell C. Prohl, *Women in the Church* (Grand Rapids: Eerdmans, 1957), 37.

6. Helen B. Andelin, *Fascinating Womanhood* (Santa Barbara: Pacific Press, 1963), 89.

7. *Gesenius's Hebrew Grammar* (London: Oxford Press), 313, 316.

8. Herbert Thoms, *Our Obstetric Heritage: The Story of Safe Childbirth* (Hamden, Conn.: Shoe String Press, 1960), 90–91.

9. Langley and Levy, *Wife Beating*, 29.

10. Del Martin, *Battered Wives* (San Francisco: Glide Publications, 1976), 26.

11. Davidson, *Conjugal Crime*, 96.

Chapter 5

1. Scanzoni and Hardesty, *All We're Meant to Be*, 102.

2. Norman Wright, *An Answer to Submission and Decision Making* (Irvine, Calif.: Harvest House, 1977), 21.

3. Louis Evans, Jr., "In Your Marriage, Who's in Charge?" *Family Life Today* (Mar. 1984): 34.

4. Wright, *Submission*, 21.

5. Ibid., 22.

6. *McLintock,* United Artists, 1963.

Chapter 6

1. Davidson, *Conjugal Crime*, 20.

2. Green and Suttor, "A Christian Response," 20.

Chapter 7

1. Norman Wright, *An Answer to Anger and Frustration* (Eugene: Harvest House, 1977), 30.

2. Monfalcone, *Coping With Abuse*, 103.

3. James Dobson, "Letting Go May Save Your Marriage," *Focus on the Family* (Oct. 1983): 3.

4. Langley and Levy, *Wife Beating*, 200, 203.

5. Lloyd Shearer, "Arrest the Wife Beaters," *Parade* (Oct. 16, 1983): 8.

6. Jennifer Baker Fleming, *Stopping Wife Abuse* (New York: Anchor Books, 1979), 21.

7. Laurence Barnhill, clinical psychologist at the Community Mental Health Center of Monroe County, Indiana, quoted by Bill Patterson, "Psychologist: Wife Beaters Aren't Bullies," *Indianapolis Star*, 30 Oct. 1980.

8. Esther Lee Olson, *No Place to Hide* (Wheaton: Tyndale, 1982), 132.

9. Ibid., 128.

10. Ibid., 142.

11. Davidson, *Conjugal Crime*, 183.

12. Lucie Prinz, "Powerless in the Suburbs," *McCall's* (Nov. 1978): 63.

13. Jennifer Parmalee, "Wife Abusers AMEND Their Ways," *Indianapolis Star*, 4 Oct. 1981.

14. Martin, *Battered Wives*, 150.

15. Davidson, *Conjugal Crime*, 190.

Chapter 8

1. Jill Blumberg Victor, "He Beat Me," *Vogue* (Jan. 1978): 185.

2. Marie Fortune, "A Commentary on Religious Issues in Family Violence," *Family Violence* (Seattle: Center for the Prevention of Sexual and Domestic Violence, 1980): 72.

3. Thomas McKenzie, "Sticks and Stones Break More Than Bones," *U.S. Catholic*, 34.

4. J. Sidlow Baxter, *Explore the Book*, vol. 3 (Grand Rapids: Zondervan, 1960), 77.

Chapter 9

1. Walker, *The Battered Woman*, 28.

2. Lenore Walker, "How Battering Happens and How to Stop It," *Battered Women*, ed., Donna Moore (Beverly Hills: Sage Publications, 1979), 77.

3. McKenzie, *U.S. Catholic*, 34.

4. Green and Suttor, "A Christian Response," 51.

DATE DUE

#47-0108 Peel Off Pressure Sensitive